Fernanda Morais

Community Therapy Rounds

Fernanda Morais

Community Therapy Rounds

ScienciaScripts

Imprint

Cover image: www.ingimage.com

This book is a translation from the original published under ISBN 978-3-8417-1203-5.

Publisher:
Sciencia Scripts
is a trademark of
Dodo Books Indian Ocean Ltd. and OmniScriptum S.R.L publishing group

120 High Road, East Finchley, London, N2 9ED, United Kingdom
Str. Armeneasca 28/1, office 1, Chisinau MD-2012, Republic of Moldova, Europe
Printed at: see last page
ISBN: 978-620-8-07971-0

ACKNOWLEDGEMENTS

To my supervisor, **Prof.ª Dr.ª Maria Djair Dias**, for all her dedication, wisdom, detachment and understanding at all times;
To the professors, Dr Francisco Arnoldo Nunes de Miranda, Drª Lenilde Duarte de Sá and Drª Maria Ferreira de Oliveira Filha, for their valuable contributions to the construction of this work;
To the Master's teachers, for showing me new ways of learning;
To my classmates, for the opportunity to exchange experiences and for welcoming me as the only doctor in the Postgraduate Nursing Programme, in the 2008/2010 class;
To the staff of the Postgraduate Nursing Programme, who were always kind enough to help me;
To the collaborators **Mountain, Water, Sky, Lake, Earth, Fire, Wind and Thunder,** for their availability and selflessness in contributing to this achievement;
Roseana Meira, João Pessoa's Secretary of Health, for her support when I needed to take time off work;
To my colleagues in Health District II, who were able to understand the challenges;
To **my parents,** who were able to understand my absences;
To my children**, Nicole, Thiago and Bianca,** for their unconditional love and support;
To Nicolau, for his understanding and support during the most difficult times I've had until I got here;
To **Maria Fernanda**, my granddaughter, for her rare patience in giving up many precious moments of our playtime;
Adriene, my friend, who encouraged me to take the Master's programme and always had words of encouragement;
To **Márcia Rique, a** friend who, with her words and attitudes, showed support and encouragement at every moment of this realisation;
To **Kerle Dayana**, friend and companion, for her support and encouragement;
Ana Paula, a friend who shared many precious moments of this work with me;
To **Fernando Lopes** and **Meihruska,** companions who supported the implementation of Community Therapy in Health Units for the professionals of the Health Strategy Teams.
Family;
To Jailton and Ewerton, my work mates at Valentina Municipal Hospital, for helping me with the computer resources;
To Karlianne and Joelma, dedicated secretaries who took care of my work schedule with such zeal that they made it possible to preserve the final moments of this achievement;
To all those who contributed to the realisation of my dream of doing a master's degree, and,
To **God**, for believing that He is the greatest force in the universe

Thank you so much!

"The intellectual's mistake consists in believing that one can know without understanding and, above all, without feeling"

(Gramsci)

SUMMARY

Community Therapy is part of a political project to transform services and the practices of health professionals. It is considered a mental health action in Primary Care that provides relief from emotional pain through moments in which feelings and experiences can be exchanged and shared, which contributes to (re)signifying life stories, as well as promoting changes in its participants. The aim of this study was to understand the changes implemented in the personal and professional dimensions of Family Health Strategy workers with experience in Community Therapies. This is a qualitative study using the methodological framework of "Thematic Oral History". The survey was carried out in the 2nd Health District, in the city of João Pessoa-PB, with eight professionals from the Family Health Strategy who took part in at least four Community Therapy sessions. The empirical data was obtained through semi-structured questions guided by a cut-off guide and analysed based on the collaborators' narratives in line with the relevant literature. The analysis allowed for the construction of two sub-themes: Community Therapy as a place of learning and Community Therapy spaces and the (re)meaning of professional practice. The study material made it possible to identify the changes in Family Health Strategy professionals in their work based on the lessons learnt from experiences in Community Therapy spaces. Community therapy can be considered a far-reaching strategy as a technology for producing care that is part of primary care from the perspective of building community-based networks for resolving conflicts for users of the Family Health Strategy and for its workers.

Key words: Community Therapy, Family Health Strategy, Labour Process.

CHAPTER 1

1. INTRODUCTION

1.1 . GETTING CLOSER TO THE OBJECT OF STUDY

In Brazil, social policies, whether public or private, have not been able to meet the needs of the population in a comprehensive way. The forces at work on the political scene have yet to prioritise reducing the suffering caused by the shortcomings of a perverse economic system, where social exclusion and marginalisation reach frightening heights in the country's poorest regions.

In the case of health, the Unified Health System (SUS), created with the promulgation of the Brazilian Constitution of 1988, ensured this achievement as a social right, having defined the expression "Health is a right of all and a duty of the State", not just as access to public health actions and services, but as the result of social and economic policies aimed at reducing the risk of disease and other illnesses (SOUSA, 2003).

It is worth considering that the health care model proposed by the SUS, representing the ideals of the Brazilian Health Reform, requires a conceptual and practical review, something capable of going beyond macro-institutional levels, allowing the sensitivity, desire and needs of the population to permeate all organisational spaces with regard to its formulation and distribution, tackling the issues of changing the work process and the participation of health workers in their ways of producing health care (CAMPINAS, 2004).

The 1990s was a remarkable period in the search for strategies aimed at ensuring that the implementation of the principles and guidelines of the SUS reached the system's user population, bringing them beyond being consumers of actions and services into a field of discussion/formulation and control/evaluation of the health policies implemented and/or being implemented.

One of the strategies adopted in this direction is the Family Health Programme (PSF), proposed by the Ministry of Health (MS) in 1994. This strategy seeks to establish bonds of co-responsibility between team professionals and the population they serve and aims to change health practices by making health promotion, prevention, care and rehabilitation actions compatible. The proposed responsibilities give health teams an intersectoral approach, based on territorialisation (FREESE, 2004).

Among the advances that have taken place over the 15 years of existence of the Family Health Strategy (ESF), which is now a state policy and one of the pillars supporting the SUS, are a number of achievements, such as expanding access to health, especially for populations historically excluded from public policies, promoting equity, improving living conditions and other achievements that are increasingly being publicised in various national and international publications (BRASIL, 2008).

However, despite the progress made in terms of its guiding principles and the decentralisation of care and management, according to the Ministry of Health (2006), the SUS still faces a series of problems, such as the existence of weaknesses both within the management of the system and within healthcare services. As a result, there are actions arising from a healthcare model centred on the complaint-conduct relationship, permeated by weak social control, making it difficult for users' rights to be respected.

The Ministry of Health recognises that low investment in the qualification of workers, especially with regard to participatory management and teamwork, few devices to encourage co-management and the appreciation and inclusion of workers and users in the health production process, coupled with the training of health workers far removed from the debate and formulation of public health policy, contribute to the persistence of this situation (BRASIL, 2006).

Also according to the Ministry of Health (2006), there is a bureaucratised and verticalised Public Health System in which a fragmented and poorly articulated care network makes it difficult for the basic network and the referral system to complement each other's actions, where professionals also act in a fragmented and isolated way amidst fragile relationships between the different professionals with precarious interaction within the teams, plus their lack of preparation to deal with the subjective dimension in care practices.

In this sense, the traditional ways of organising health work based on the logic of the professions have been insufficient to guarantee humanised and comprehensive care, resulting in fragmented thinking and acting in the health system as a whole.

The current health care model is characterised as a "producer of procedures", since the production of services is based on the clinic run by the doctor, and given that the ESF organises its actions according to the logic of health surveillance as a priority, its significant potential to reverse the hegemonic medical model is diminished (MERHY, 1998).

In this process of building the SUS, the commitment to the changes needed to reverse the care model poses challenges for all social segments committed to defending life, as it implies recognising that building a new, more humanised health model presupposes expanding the care dimension and, by this logic, the development of actions and the functioning of services still have several gaps.

Structured as a proposal to deal with the process of reorganising the primary care network, the ESF would also be a strategy for reorienting the entire SUS, as envisioned by its formulators. It relies on a number of professionals, such as doctors, nurses, nursing technicians, community workers and others, but each one does their job separately, without direct co-operation (MEHRY, 2002, SOUSA, 2003).

In this way, the organisation of the work process of primary care professionals remains distant from the world of users' needs, and discussions about this fragility are frequent, as mentioned by Campos (2003), who believes that only by changing the way health workers relate to users will it be possible to comply with the constitutional precepts that guarantee the effective right to health for all Brazilians.

Public policies must develop actions that guarantee health according to the needs of each user, and not centralise assistance to the disease, but must direct care towards reducing the risks, eradicating the causes, as well as treating and recovering the damage. One of the existing challenges in society for managers, health workers and social movements is the consolidation of a mental health network made up of a set of health actions and services that consider the subject in psychological distress according to their singularity, complexity, integrality and socio-cultural insertion, creating bonds, humanising care, seeking to guarantee the right of citizenship (BRASIL, 2007).

As for mental health care in primary care, this component is still fragile, as most health services do not offer basic guidance to the population, such as ways of dealing with crises, emotional suffering, as well as the importance of emotional and social relationships in the life of each person and the community (FERREIRA FILHA; DIAS, 2007).

Successful experiences, which have been carried out in several Brazilian municipalities in all states, indicate the development of basic mental health actions by ESF teams as a complementary and fundamental possibility in the consolidation of the community-based health care model, where health promotion and disease prevention are considered strategic actions for maintaining a better quality of life.

Among the experiences focused on mental health in primary care, Community Therapy has emerged on the national scene as a wide-reaching care technology with low operating costs that can be adopted by Family Health Teams (ESFs) in the day-to-day running of health units and in the community to build supportive social networks, minimising the emotional suffering of the population arising from problems related to poverty, migration, abandonment, insecurity and low esteem (FERREIRA FILHA; DIAS, 2007).

In May 2006, Ministerial Order No. 971 was published, approving the National Policy for Integrative and Complementary Practices (PNPIC) in the SUS. This policy responds, above all, to the need to know, support, incorporate and implement experiences that have already been developed in the public network of many municipalities and states, including those in the fields of Traditional Chinese Medicine - Acupuncture, Homeopathy, Phytotherapy, Anthroposophic Medicine and Thermalism-Crenotherapy.

Considering the person in their global dimension without losing sight of their singularity, the PNPIC corroborates the promotion of comprehensive health care, seeking to bring together and integrate health actions in a multidisciplinary way. The search to expand the range of health actions has, in the implementation of the PNPIC in the SUS, opened up possibilities for access to services that were previously restricted to private practice (BRASIL, 2008).

By acting in the fields of disease prevention and health promotion, maintenance and recovery based on a humanised care model and centred on the individual's integrality, the PNIPIC contributes to strengthening primary care and the fundamental principles of the SUS. In this sense, this policy should be seen as another step in the process of implementing the SUS, and it is precisely as a Complementary Practice that Community Therapy is included in the SUS (ANDRADE *et al.*, 2009).

Currently, the Ministry of Health recognises and includes Community Therapy as an integrative and complementary health practice, especially in relation to the mental health of people in the community. With a view to expanding the use of this care technology, which has been expanding as a group therapeutic procedure to promote health and prevent illness, the Ministry of Health intends to support the qualification of health professionals and community leaders to promote social support networks in Primary Care (BRASIL, 2008).

In the municipality of João Pessoa-PB, Community Therapy has been used in a pioneering way since August 2004, as part of the Extension Project carried out in the Mangabeira neighbourhood, coordinated by teachers from the Postgraduate Nursing Programme and the Department of Public Health Nursing and Psychiatry at the Federal University of Paraíba-UFPB (GUIMARÃES; FERREIRA FILHA, 2006).

The teachers involved in the above-mentioned project say:

> Our concern has also been to focus on the training and qualification of human resources to work in mental health care in primary health care, where nurses are an essential element of this practice and Community Therapy has been used as an instrument to reflect on the work process of professionals in family health teams (FERREIRA FILHA; DIAS, 2007).

The Municipal Health Department (SMS) of João Pessoa-PB, since the municipal administration of 2005, has prioritised in its political project the production of comprehensive, humanised and quality care, as well as adopting the guidelines of

Permanent Health Education, Matriciamento and Acolhimento as strategies to achieve its objective (JOÃO PESSOA, 2006).

In order to achieve this goal, the João Pessoa-PB SMS recognises the need to invest in the qualification of the group of managers of the various services and directorates and, among the strategies adopted in this direction, it is betting on permanent health education and the constitution of reference teams for matrix support to the work of the Family Health Teams as devices for the desired transformation, i.e. the consolidation of the local SUS.

At this juncture, the João Pessoa-PB SMS, recognising that Community Therapy has the power to be configured as a mental health care device in primary care, promoted a training course in 2007 for 63 workers, involving the various health occupations in the primary care network and the Psychosocial Care Centres (CAPS), as well as management representatives.

Given the opportunity to take part in training in Community Therapy, I developed an interest in this subject based on my experience as a manager in the role of Director of Health District II, one of the five Health Districts in João Pessoa-PB, from January 2007 to February 2009. This experience sparked my desire to try to understand the difficulties that the ESF teams were going through. I consider the difficulties to be those arising from the challenges and conflicts in transforming their practice and developing work involving the various professionals, creating real possibilities for changing the current working conditions, guaranteeing the principle of comprehensive health care for people and the community.

Recognising that Community Therapy can be a tool capable of facilitating the promotion of transformative actions in people's lives, in 2008 I started conducting Community Therapy circles with the ESFs that had difficulties organising their work processes, based on the identification of the district technical team's matrix supporters. From this experience of conducting weekly Community Therapy circles, I realised from the participants' reports that some change was taking place with these professionals.

So, having joined the Postgraduate Programme in Nursing and having studied Community Therapy, it was possible to get closer to the theory and, from there, I came up with the following guiding questions for this study: was the participation of ESF professionals in Community Therapy circles able to bring about changes in their work process? If so, how do ESF professionals identify these changes? What are the most significant changes?

The study is linked to a larger project entitled: *Community Therapy in the context of the SUS*, coordinated by professors from the Postgraduate Programme in Nursing and the Department of Public Health Nursing and Psychiatry at the Federal University of Paraíba (UFPB), as part of the line of research Policy and Practices in Health and Nursing.

This study is of significant importance because it seeks to deepen the investigation of a topic that has been arousing interest among undergraduate and postgraduate nursing students at UFPB, thanks to the encouragement of the coordinating and supervising professors. As an example of scientific production as a result of this line of research, we can mention the development of dissertations by Guimarães (2006), Holanda (2006), Oliveira (2008) and Rocha (2009), linked to the theme of Community Therapy, with positive results.

We would also add that the results of this study could contribute to building knowledge about the experiences that have been made with this care tool in Primary Care, with a view to building social support networks in line with the principles of the SUS.

1.2 OBJECTIVES

1.2.1 GENERAL OBJECTIVE

- To understand the changes that have taken place in the personal and professional dimensions of workers in the Family Health Strategy as a result of their experience in Community Therapy circles.

1.2.2 SPECIFIC OBJECTIVES

- To identify the changes that have taken place in the personal dimension of Family Health Strategy workers who use Community Therapy groups;
- To identify the changes that have taken place in the professional dimension of Family Health Strategy workers who use Community Therapy groups.

CHAPTER 2

2. THEORETICAL FRAMEWORK

2.1 SYSTEMIC INTEGRATIVE COMMUNITY THERAPY: CONCEPTS, DESIGN AND THEORETICAL ASSUMPTIONS

Systemic Integrative Community Therapy was developed by Prof Dr Adalberto de Paula Barreto, a professor in the Department of Social Medicine at the Federal University of Ceará (UFC), who has been working with this subject since 1987. The professor is internationally recognised for being the creator and promoter of the technique, which is present in 27 Brazilian states with 30 training centres throughout the country (BRASIL, 2008).

Therapy is a word of Greek origin (*therapeia*) which means to welcome, to be warm, to serve, to attend to. So a therapist is someone who welcomes and cares for others in a warm way.

The word community is made up of two other words: COMMON + UNITY, i.e. what people have in common. Among other affinities, they share suffering, exclusion, seek solutions and overcome difficulties (BARRETO, 2008).

The aforementioned author describes Systemic Community Therapy:

> Systems thinking tells us that crises and problems can only be understood and resolved if they are perceived as integrated parts of a complex network, which connect and interconnect people as a whole. We are a whole, in which each part influences and interferes with the other. Therefore, if human suffering is a result of the socio-economic, political and social macro-context, the responses must also be systemic, mobilising resources from the Brazilian multiculture (BARRETO, 2008, p.37).

According to the same author, Integrative Systemic Community Therapy considers that all the living forces in the community should play an active role in promoting health, integrating knowledge from the most diverse socio-cultural contexts and expanding solidarity networks to promote health and citizenship. In this way, culture should be seen as a valuable resource that can be mobilised and articulated with other knowledge in the quest to tackle social problems and build a fairer, more democratic society (BARRETO, 2008).

Community therapy is characterised by being a space for talking, listening and building bonds, with the aim of offering support to individuals and families experiencing stress and psychological suffering. Its function is not to solve people's problems, but to create a dynamic that enables the creation of a support network for those who are suffering (BARRETO, 2008).

Community therapy can also be found in countries such as France, Switzerland and Uruguay, and in Brazil it takes place in all the states through a collective that has already exceeded 13,000 community therapists trained through partnerships with the Brazilian Association of Community Therapy (ABRATECOM, 2009).

Community therapy can be defined as a community space where life experiences and knowledge are shared in a horizontal and circular way, in a warm and welcoming environment in which everyone becomes co-responsible for finding solutions and overcoming the challenges of everyday life (BARRETO, 2008).

The basic characteristics of Community Therapy are the discussion and implementation of community-based preventive mental health work. It emphasises group work as an instrument of social aggregation and, based on this dynamic, proposes the gradual creation of social awareness so that individuals can discover the transformative therapeutic potential acquired from human suffering.

According to Barreto (2008), Community Therapy has the following objectives:

> Valuing the internal dynamics of each individual, strengthening their autonomy; reinforcing individual and collective self-esteem; rediscovering and increasing confidence in each individual through self-knowledge; enhancing the role of the family and its network of relationships; promoting feelings of unity and identification with local cultural values on the part of individuals, families and groups; favour community development by restoring and strengthening social ties; value traditional cultural institutions and practices; make communication possible between scientific knowledge and popular knowledge; and encourage participation as a fundamental requirement for promoting collective awareness and encouraging people to be agents of their own transformation (BARRETO, 2008, p. 39). 39).

Conducted by a pair of therapists, the Community Therapy circles take place with the participants in a circle, guided by the systematisation of a technique that comprises six stages: welcoming, choice of theme, contextualisation, problematisation, rituals of aggregation and positive connotation, and evaluation (BARRETO, 2008).

1. Welcome: This lasts approximately seven minutes, with the aim of bringing the participants closer to the group, making them feel comfortable and well settled, defining the purpose of the meeting, encouraging people to celebrate life and their achievements, clarifying the rules of operation (keeping quiet to listen to the speaker; talking about one's own experience; not giving advice, speeches or sermons; suggesting a song, telling a proverb or even a joke that has some connection with the topic under discussion, and, respecting each person's life story), proposing an interactive dynamic and passing on the conduct to the other therapist on the team.

2. Choice of topic: lasting around ten minutes, it consists of five procedures:

2.1. Therapist's words: begins with the therapist greeting the participants, then announces that it's time to talk about what's causing the restlessness, insomnia or worry, referring to the phrase: "When the mouth is silent, the organs speak, but when the mouth speaks the organs heal"; he continues by encouraging people to talk about everyday worries and not to bring up any big secrets; he asks those who want to speak to identify themselves by saying their name and what the problem is in a few words, because then the group chooses just one of the situations presented to be worked on at the time.

2.2. Presentation of the issues: The stage continues with the therapist asking: "Who would like to speak today?" And, as the presentation of the problems is being made by the people who decide to speak, the therapist should record the names of the people and the problem presented and, before passing the floor to the next person interested in speaking, restitute it with the question: "Let me see if I've understood your problem, and if I'm wrong, please correct me or add to it".

2.3. The group identifies with the themes presented: At this point, the community therapist summarises each of the problems noted and asks the group to answer the question, "Which problem touched you the most?" When he hears the answer, he asks: "Why?" And after around 20 per cent of the participants have spoken, justifying their identification, he moves on to choose the one that will be explored in greater depth, proposing that those present take a vote.

2.4. Voting: This is preceded by the clarification that everyone can vote (except the

therapist), but only on one topic, and the votes are counted as the group raises its hand while the topics are put to the vote. It's recommended to start the vote with the topic that didn't show any significance, and therefore little identification with the group.
2.5. Acknowledgement: Once the vote is over, the theme to be worked on is announced and the group begins to delve deeper. It is made clear that the therapist appreciates those who did not have their topic chosen, thanks them for the trust they have placed in the group and makes himself available for some guidance if they wish, at the end of the Community Therapy, or even reinforcing and instilling confidence to re-present the situation in other meetings if this is the case and of interest to the proposer and the group.
3. Contextualisation: lasting around fifteen minutes, this stage comprises two moments: One concerning the information and the other about the motto: this is the moment for the participants to understand the chosen problem. It consists of two procedures:
3.1. Information: The person who has had the theme chosen will explain, tell about their suffering and everyone can ask questions that help them understand it in its context. These questions help the protagonist to reflect on the situation and help the therapist to develop the theme.
3.2. Motto: a key question that will allow the group to reflect on their experience, after which the therapist thanks the protagonist and asks them to be attentive to the speech of the others present.
4. Problematisation: at this stage, which lasts an average of 45 minutes, the therapist presents the MOTE to the group, at which point the protagonist listens and remains silent. The motto is used to motivate the people in the group to express their experiences, which are then written down to finalise the Community Therapy. During the circle, the therapist realises that the problematisation has achieved its objective by saturating the participants' speeches. At this point, he asks the participants to stand and asks them to form a circle, placing their hands on each other's shoulders. This brings the discussion to a close.
5. Closing: rituals of aggregation and positive connotation: this stage, which lasts an average of ten minutes, takes place with people standing, feeling close to each other, in an affective atmosphere where the therapist tries to give a positive connotation, i.e. highlight what was positive about the story told in the group, always valuing the person as the human being they are. The person who has had the theme worked on will receive a positive connotation from the therapist who then invites the group to do the same, saying what they have learnt or something that has touched them. To finish, the group is asked to sing a song, or chant a religious song, recite a poem or use another technique that allows the collective dimension to be aroused and strengthened.
6. Evaluation: carried out right after the end of each meeting, this is the moment when the team of therapists evaluates how the Community Therapy circle was conducted and the impact of the meeting on each person, taking into account the different stages aimed at improving the practice (BARRETO, 2008).

Theoretically, Community Therapy has built its identity on five main axes: Systemic Thinking, Communication Theory, Cultural Anthropology, Paulo Freire's Pedagogy and Resilience, as set out below:

a) Systems Thinking

According to Munhoz and Malanga (2002), systemic thinking makes it possible to understand the relationships between the various elements of a system and to know it as a whole, analysing its parts and the interaction between them, developing a contextual understanding. As well as contextualising the phenomena taking place, a systemic approach considers relationships and mutual implications to be important and respects diversity and unity at the same time.

According to Capra (2000), the systemic conception sees the world from a perspective of relationships and integration, valuing the whole and its relationships with its constituent parts, so that the whole is the result of its interaction with its constituents and not the sum of them. The vision of reality defended by this thinking is based on an awareness of the state of interrelatedness and essential interdependence of all physical, biological, psychological, social and cultural phenomena.

With this in mind, Pasello (2007) emphasises that by seeking to understand the whole, it becomes possible to understand the parts that make it up. Not just a simple sum of the parts, but the articulation between them, with their own characteristics, peculiarities and needs, which will become a unique whole, with a specific dynamic.

It is worth adding that the above author emphasises that all aspects of the different types of knowledge must have the same value, making it possible to create a dynamic balance between the articulated parts (PASELLO, 2007).

According to Barreto (2008), a system can be defined as a complex of elements in interdependent interactions that organises a whole and has its own functioning. A family can be thought of as a system and the relationships its members maintain with each other and with other human organisations form other configurations that are called subsystems.

According to Bertalanffy (1968 *apud* BARRETO, 2008), it is possible to identify some basic characteristics in the system:

Systems are totalising or globalising and even if they are made up of various elements or parts, they function as a whole, with total interdependence. Therefore, you can only understand an element of the system, or one of its parts, if, when you look at it, you understand the system as a whole, since the whole is more important than the sum of the parts, and so, to understand a system, it is not enough to understand the parts in isolation;

The members of a system are organised around common meanings and interdependent relationships, in which the union of the elements is not by chance. This union follows a logic of its own, because there is a kind of affinity, of identification, albeit sometimes unconscious, but based on records of memories impregnated in the body and mind;

The system is endowed with a capacity for self-protection, self-equilibrium, self-development and self-transcendence, because it is the system's duty to fight to maintain its organisation and autonomy, protecting itself from internal and external aggressions and seeking self-preservation. Every community is like this, as are families and individuals;

Circular causality replaces the linear cause-effect relationship with circularity, and thus feeds on information and energies that circulate with the notion that everything and everyone involved in the same context are related with a commitment to changing all the elements for the transformation of the systemic whole;

Purpose is perhaps the most important point of the systemic approach, as it states that the elements of a system interact motivated by a common goal. Without a common goal, the health of the system is compromised, be it the individual's system, or the family, social, community or any other system.

Every problem situation needs to be understood from the context in which it occurs as part of a complex whole full of ramifications involving the biological, psychological and social. The systemic approach is always interactive, and it is necessary to be aware of this globality in order to understand the mechanisms of self-regulation, protection and growth of social systems, and to experience the notion of co-responsibility (BARRETO, 2008).

Thus, in Community Therapy circles, when a problem is exposed, based on the contribution of systemic thinking, the social and cultural contexts are valued and interconnected, making it possible to understand them based on the insertion of the life stories of those involved.

In view of the above, Barreto (2008) gives an example:

> At this point, questions are asked that help to clarify what happened, to better situate the events, thus allowing the problem to be understood in its global context and, at the same time, enabling the person speaking to better organise their ideas, feelings and emotions (BARRETO, 2008, p. 70).

b) Communication Theory

According to Littlejohnn (1998), communication is one of the most complex and important clusters present in human behaviour. Through communication, you can understand the world, relate to others and transform yourself and the reality that surrounds you. Community Therapy is based on Watzlawick's Communication Theory (1967), which states that communication has five basic rules:

The **first rule** states that all behaviour is communication and all communication, including communication cues, in an impersonal context, affects behaviour. Most of the time, communication through gestures and attitudes occurs unconsciously and unintentionally. That's why every sign or symptom has communicative value and always hides something important.

The **second rule** says that all communication has two components: the content (or message) and the relationship between the interlocutors. The content is everything that is communicated with words or gestures, and when a person communicates with another, they are offering a definition of themselves and expecting a response. That's why the verbal or gestural response is like a mirror that allows the person to recognise themselves.

In view of the above rule, Barreto (2008) corroborates when he says: People don't communicate just to transmit information, but mainly to gain awareness of their own self.

The **third rule** states that all communication depends on punctuation. Thus, problems arising from punctuation occur when the interlocutor becomes convinced that their belief is the only correct one in the world, which can trigger conflict. It is therefore necessary to get the punctuation of communication sequences right, otherwise a crisis will ensue.

The **fourth rule** is that all communication has two modes of expression: verbal communication (spoken and written language) and non-verbal communication (analogue or gestural). For Barreto (2008), for communication to be complete, it needs a combination of the two languages mentioned, and he adds: There can only be growth where communication is clear, without duplication, without contradiction, without double meanings.

In this sense, the same author states that the community therapist needs to be careful not to allow double communication to take place between the participants in Community Therapy circles, as communication needs to unambiguously confirm each person's identity in order for growth to take place.

Finally, the **fifth rule** is that communication can be: symmetrical, based on similarity (it happens between people who live in close proximity and act in imitation of each other) or complementary, based on what is different (despite having different roles, the partners try to complement each other's behaviour).

According to Barreto (2008), communication theory points to the fact that communication between people is the element that unites individuals, families and society. The author states that the richness and variety of communication possibilities between people invites us to go beyond words, to understand each human being's desperate search for the awareness of existing and belonging, of being confirmed and recognised as a subject and citizen.

For this author, the person who takes part in the Community Therapy circle, when they talk about their suffering, reveals their fantasies and expresses their emotions, while at the same time freeing themselves from what oppresses them. This allows the group to reflect on the roots of human suffering and to outline practical, curative and preventative solutions.

According to Barreto (2008), it is essential to pay attention to the different modes of communication expressed in Community Therapy circles:

> [...] When a person decides to talk about their suffering, their anguish, they are not just expressing a complaint or verbal information. Through their tears, their broken voice and their silence, they communicate the suffering that annihilates them, the fragility that inhabits them and the fear that dominates them. In turn, the group that listens to her ends up echoing what they have heard. Those who identify themselves can finally speak of what inhabited them in silence. Listening arouses the desire for solidarity, awakens compassion and, in this way, the first steps towards building a community of solidarity are sketched out. From that moment on, the person doesn't feel alone. They already have someone to share with (BARRETO, 2008, p. 54).

c) Cultural Anthropology

For Corrêa (2000), anthropology studies issues relating to human diversity and began in the 19th century. Anthropologists generally investigate the ways in which human behaviour develops, seeking to fully describe socio-cultural phenomena.

According to Boas (2004), culture defines everything that human beings do: the way they live, eat, dress and follow religious rituals. Learned behaviour is passed down through the generations and is not instinctive behaviour, but something that results from behavioural mechanisms introjected by the individual.

Culture, according to Laplantine's (1995) definition, is the set of behaviours and knowledge characteristic of a human group. These activities are acquired through a learning process and transmitted to all its members through the processes of contact, diffusion, interaction and acculturation. The author also states:

> [...] Trapped in a single culture, we are not only blind to that of others, but short-sighted when it comes to our own. The experience of otherness makes us see what we can't imagine because of our difficulty in fixing our attention on what is habitual and believing that we are one possible culture among many others (LAPLANTINE, 1995, p. 21).

Cultural anthropology, according to Barreto (2005), emphasises cultural values as important factors in the formation of individual and group identity, understanding it as an area that provides support for building social networks that include intersectoral and interinstitutional actions, valuing local resources, strengthening bonds and supporting family dynamics.

The same author states that if culture is seen as a value, a resource that can be articulated with other knowledge, it makes it possible to recognise the richness of the coexistence of various cultural elements and that this resource can enhance the construction of a more fraternal and just society.

Barreto (2008) compares culture to an invisible web that integrates and unites individuals in the search for collective solutions to everyday concerns. Solutions cannot be found without the support of the cultural values inherited from the ancestors that make up Brazilian society: indigenous, African, European and Asian. The same author says:

> Brazilian society is made up of an enormous cultural plurality, and there is therefore a great diversity of perceptions of the world and how to care for it. Failure to respect this diversity masks an unbearable neo-colonialism, which excludes other approaches, other readings of other knowledge constructed in other cultural universes (BARRETO, 2008, p. 290).

In this sense, cultural anthropology, as a theoretical framework for Community Therapy, seeks to understand the meanings that individuals themselves attribute to their behaviour, and is of great interest for everyday life, its challenges, joys and habits. Therefore, in Community Therapy, healing involves recovering the roots and cultural values that awaken in people and social groups a sense of security and a feeling of belonging, in other words, belonging to a culture that has been denied by society, but which can be experienced in the collective space (BARRETO, 2008). This author adds:

> [...] If the cultural elements that give people and groups their identity are destroyed, the same thing will happen as if the web that sustains the spider were destroyed. Just as the spider needs its web to feed, multiply and live, people need the support of their culture, they need to recognise themselves in it, love it and defend it. Without the web that supports them, they have no way of living (BARRETO, 2008, p. 243-244).

There is no hierarchy in culture, so in Community Therapy circles, people have the opportunity to learn from each other in an environment in which culture, being the framework of their identities, can act as a stimulus for participants to seek solutions to their problems, and to make some effort towards organising themselves as a group and building their own citizenship (BARRETO, 2008).

d) Paulo Freire's Pedagogy

Pedagogical aspects of Paulo Freire's theory, for whom teaching is not just a transfer of knowledge from the educator to the learner, but an exercise in dialogue, exchange and reciprocity, underpin the practice of Community Therapy as a space for collective learning. In this approach, the educational process is horizontal and requires, so common sense, humility and tolerance.

According to Barreto (2008), Community Therapy, as a pedagogical tool, is based on Freire's (2000) framework, which reflects that, in relation to the educator, it is essential that there be:

> Respect for students' knowledge; criticality; aesthetics and ethics; embodiment of words by example; risk, acceptance of the new and rejection of any form of discrimination; critical reflection on practice; recognition and assumption of cultural identity, awareness of unfinishedness; recognition of being conditioned; respect for the autonomy of the student's being; common sense; humility; tolerance and struggle in defence of educators' rights; apprehension of reality; joy and hope; conviction that change is possible; curiosity; security, professional competence and generosity; commitment; understanding that education is a form of intervention in the world; freedom and authority; conscious decision making; recognition that

> education is dialogical; willingness to engage in dialogue; knowing how to listen and wanting to do well by the students (BARRETO, 2008, p. 280). 280).

The aforementioned profile brings the role of the educator closer to that of the community therapist, since it understands Community Therapy as a pedagogical instrument that places teaching as a practice of dialogue, with time to speak and to listen, seeking to theorise about reality from the expression of the problems experienced, rescuing life stories as a source of knowledge, respect and acceptance of diversity, accepting and understanding the human being as an unfinished being, and perceiving them as a historical subject, inviting both to a continuous doing and redoing, acting and reflecting (BARRETO, 2008).

The same author also says that in Community Therapy circles, everyone is the doctor of their own experience. In this way, the skills and competences of each participant are valued according to the reality and context in which they are inserted.

e) Resilience

According to Ferreira (1999), *resilience* is a word derived from the English *resilience*, used in physics as a property by which the energy stored in a deformed body is returned when the stress causing an elastic deformation ceases.

According to Wlash (2005), resilience is an active process of resistance, restructuring and growth in response to crisis. For Barreto (2005), resilience is a process in which the individual overcomes a deficiency by transforming it into competence. Resilient people highly value the bonds of support and encouragement they receive and, by sharing their experiences, they reinforce their self-esteem, strengthen interpersonal bonds and improve their autonomy.

According to Barreto (2008), crises are disorders and disorganisations that occur at certain times in the lives of individuals, families, social groups, institutions and society. They can show signs such as the individual's, family's or social group's inability to solve their problems, a lack of creativity, a tendency to resort to extremist attitudes and a loss of direction (not knowing what to do).

From this perspective, the importance of the crisis as an opportunity for learning as well as personal, family and community growth is emphasised, as it makes it possible to reflect on mistakes made, review relationships, seek new ways of acting and relating (BARRETO, 2008).

It is worth highlighting what Barreto (2008) adds:

> Crisis will always be our eternal companion in our evolutionary process. It is a necessary evil, because it allows us to leave behind what we no longer need. Many crises can be overcome alone. When people can't find a way out on their own in the midst of the storm, the support of a friend or the community can be of great value (BARRETO, 2008, p. 127).

During Community Therapy sessions, being able to talk about pain can be an important factor in rebuilding life. A well-utilised crisis can turn chaos into raw material for human growth, for the growth of the group itself and of an entire community. For this reason, Barreto (2008) states that life experience, shortcomings and suffering, when overcome, are transformed into sensitivity and competence, leading us to actions that repair other suffering.

Still corroborating the aforementioned author, when he emphasises that:

> A word, a gesture of support can make the difference between those who fail and those who succeed. We have observed that as people share

> their suffering in Community Therapy, they transform their feelings and enable a (re)signification of the traumatic events, weaving social bonds and generating a sense of belonging to the group (BARRETO, 2008, p. 100).

In this way, Community Therapy enables the creation of a web of social relationships that enhances the exchange of experiences, the recovery of skills and the overcoming of adversity based on the formation of socio-emotional resources and the conquest of individual and collective power (DIAS; FERREIRA FILHA, 2007).

Over the years, Community Therapy has demonstrated its efficiency in promoting self-esteem and preventing mental disorders, as well as helping people to recover affective and social bonds, and is considered to be an instrument that facilitates aggregation and social inclusion (BARRETO, 2005).

The co-participatory model of Community Therapy is based on people's competence. People who have problems also have solutions. By valuing individual experiences, recognising each person's contribution and reinforcing the self-esteem of those who share their skills, it helps to create and strengthen bonds between people/groups/community (BARRETO, 2005).

During the Community Therapy circles, the aim is to recover the knowledge produced by the experience and allow it to be socialised, verbalised, not with the aim of identifying shortcomings, but above all with the aim of highlighting what has been done to overcome or confront them. It's not a question of rejecting academic knowledge, but, as Barreto says:

> Community therapy is based on people's competences and the knowledge produced by experience. Its participants are considered true experts in overcoming suffering. Their life stories have made them experts in overcoming obstacles and producing knowledge that is generally ignored by academia (BARRETO, 2008 p. 103).

2.2 HEALTH WORK PROCESS

According to Pires (2000), health work is essential to human life and stands out in the service sector in the sphere of non-material production. It does not result in a material product that is independent of the production process and can be sold on the market. The product is inseparable from the process that produces it, being the very realisation of the activity.

Unlike industry, in the case of healthcare, the worker who provides care is the producer of health, and in this condition interacts with the consumer (user) while producing the procedures. What's more, they will be consumed by the user at the very moment they are produced, thus determining a fundamental characteristic of health work, which is that it is relational, i.e. it happens through the relationship between worker and user, whether individual or collective (FRANCO, 2003).

Various professional categories carry out their activities according to the piecemeal division of labour, such as nursing, for example, where there is fragmentation of tasks under the coordination of higher-level professionals (RIBEIRO, 2004).

In practice, health work, in order to be effective, must respond to a configuration that is not just technical, but as a practice of relationships between the worker and the user, as a practice between human beings, who are also constituted by relationships with others and with the world, producing and reproducing themselves and their environment (FRANCO, 2003).

Health work refers to a complex and dynamic world in which users seek to solve health problems with workers on a daily basis. The moment when the work is carried out is characterised by an encounter between worker and user, determining the consumption of what is produced at the exact moment of its production and this determines a fundamental characteristic of health work, which is that it is relational, an expression of living work that gives meaning to the work in act (MERHY, 2002, FRANCO, 2003).

Merhy (2003) goes on to say that:

> Any approach by a health worker to a user-patient is produced through live work in action, in a process of relationships, i.e. there is an encounter between two "people", who act on each other, and in which a game of expectations and productions operates, intersubjectively creating some interesting moments, such as the following: moments of speaking, listening and interpreting, in which the intentions that these people have in this encounter are accepted or not; moments of complicity, in which accountability is produced around the problem that is going to be faced; moments of reliability and hope, in which relationships of bonding and acceptance are produced (MERHY, 2003, p. p.). 77).

This moment when a health worker meets a user, defined by Merhy (1997) as an intercessory space, is a unique opportunity for each worker to make the most of their power to effectively solve users' health problems. This creative and creative function, which can characterise health services based on unique relationships, is operated by soft technologies, a territory where live work in action is inscribed. Live work in act is work that takes place at the very moment it is realised in the immediate production of the service (FRANCO; MERHY, 1999).

According to Franco (2006), health work is not a category isolated from the productive and relational context. It is a dynamic process crossed by as many interests as there are subjects interacting in the production of care.

It is worth pointing out that, at the same time as subjects organise their work processes, as they work, they produce the world in which they are inserted, and themselves, in processes of subjectivation, which affect them and therefore become products of their own experiences (FRANCO; MERHY, 2007).

According to Cecílio (2001), it is possible to work on the integrality of care within a health service as a result of the effort and confluence of the various skills of a multi-professional team, with the commitment and concern always prevailing to listen as best as possible to the health needs brought by the person who comes to the service with a specific demand. This author states that:

> In this situation, it would be up to the team to have the sensitivity and preparation to decode and know how to meet users' needs in the best possible way. To this end, the whole emphasis of management, the organisation of care and the training of workers should be on a greater capacity to listen to and meet health needs, rather than pure and simple adherence to any model of care given a priori (CECÍLIO, 2001, p. 4).

In the current medical-hegemonic care model, the flow of care in a Basic Health Unit is geared towards medical consultations. The work process in this case lacks the interaction of knowledge and practices necessary for comprehensive health care. A central issue here is the fact that this situation will only be achieved through the efforts of each individual worker and the team as a whole (CECÍLIO, 2001).

In the current mode of health production, the use of hard technologies (those inscribed in machines and instruments) still prevails, to the detriment of soft-hard technologies (defined by technical knowledge) and soft technologies (the technologies of relationships) for user care. Changing the care model requires an inversion of the care technologies to be used in health production (MERHY, 1998).

According to Ayres (2005), on the other hand, work processes operate in intercessory relationships between workers and between workers and users, to the extent that both form an encounter in which they place themselves as actors/subjects in the production of care.

Betting on the production of care in which the work process of professionals is re-signified through the encounter of intersubjectivities is a possibility for confronting social inequalities and re-constructing the autonomy of subjects (PIRES; DEMO, 2006).

In reality, thinking about the integrality of care can mean incorporating the different needs of users and the context in which these health needs are produced into the production of health care. In this way, it is a great challenge for human beings to combine work and care, since the two are not opposed; on the contrary, they are compounded in that they mutually limit and at the same time complement each other. It is a mistake to oppose one dimension to the other, because together they constitute the integrality of human experience, linked to materiality on the one hand and spirituality on the other (BOFF, 2008).

In this sense, the same author states that the rescue of care does not come at the expense of work, but through a different way of understanding and carrying out work. To do this, human beings need to turn in on themselves and discover their way of being cared for. Only human beings have feelings, the capacity to be moved, to get involved, to affect and to feel affected, and so, based on this reasoning, he adds:

> It is the feeling that unites us with things and involves us with people. It's the feeling that produces enchantment in the face of the greatness of the heavens, arouses veneration in the face of the complexity of Mother Earth and nurtures tenderness in the face of the fragility of a newborn baby [...] It's the feeling that makes people, things and situations important to us. This deep feeling is called care. Only that which has passed through an emotion, which has evoked a deep feeling and provoked care in us, leaves indelible marks and remains permanently (BOFF, 2008, p. 100).

For Ayres (2004), once the implications of care have been taken on board, as the technical dimensions of health practices on the part of the health professional, the dialogical dimension of the encounter with the other becomes relevant in their daily lives, abandoning the possibility of listening to themselves and making themselves heard.

According to Bertoncini (2000), the work environment in which family health teams operate produces alienation, impotence, stress, conflicts, power struggles, fear, insecurity and low self-esteem, thus jeopardising the chances of changing the current conditions and guaranteeing the principle of comprehensive care.

For Pinheiro and Guisardi (2008), the search for care has currently been unequivocally identified as one of the main demands for healthcare in Brazilian society. It is a demand that emerges as a critique of things, institutions, practices and discourses in health, according to the authors, who add:

> When we refer to the notion of care, we don't understand it as a level of attention in the health system or as a simplified technical procedure, but as an integral action that has meanings and senses geared towards understanding health as a right to be. It is treating, respecting, welcoming and attending to human beings in their suffering, which is largely the result of their social fragility (PINHEIRO; GUIZARDI, 2008, p. 23).

Still according to Ayres (2005), caring, in the sense of "treating that is", involves technical competences and tasks, but is not restricted to them; it more richly embodies what the practical task of collective health should be than treating, curing or controlling.

To this end, it is pertinent to revisit the concept of comprehensiveness as one of the pillars underpinning the creation of the SUS, a principle enshrined in the 1988 Federal Constitution, the fulfilment of which can help guarantee the quality of health care (CAMPOS, 2003).

The principle of comprehensiveness cannot be understood simply as a synonym for guaranteeing access to all levels of the health services system. Integrality is, in fact, a much deeper principle. According to Mattos (2004), at least three meanings can be identified for comprehensiveness: that it is a set of meanings applied to the characteristics of health policies and the scope of government responses, in the sense of articulating preventive actions with care demands; a set of meanings relating to aspects of the organisation of health services and, finally, attributes relating to health practices.

In this way, the problems identified in the ESF's daily routine require a better adaptation of health practices and a reassessment of users' real needs, using soft technologies. Observing and discussing how relationships are built up between professionals and their users is a promising field for the possibility of changes in "doing health" (MEHRY *et al.*, 2003).

The reorganisation of work processes has emerged as the main issue to be tackled in order to change health services, in order to make them operate in a way that focuses on the user and their needs, because although there has been investment in education since the principles of the Brazilian health reform were established, most of the time care practices remain the same, structured by a work process that operates on the basis of hierarchical relationships, care remains cursory and distant from the needs of users (FRANCO, 2007).

For Franco (2007), some questions have always been with us, for example:

> Why is it that despite all the efforts in education, most of the time care practices remain the same, structured by a work process that operates on the basis of hierarchical relationships, care remains cursory and workers are sheltered in their small space of know-how, showing great difficulty in interacting and forming a multi-professional practice? Why does a fragmented work process persist in the health services, along Taylorist lines, with knowledge that is isolated from each other, where it is difficult for members of the same team to interact, above all, under the values and culture of a clinic whose reference is the old (Flexnerian) model, which survives the countless appeals made in the various education strategies (training, revisions/updates, etc.) for health workers? (FRANCO, 2007, p. 3).

When the work process is commanded by living labour, the worker has a great deal of freedom to be creative, to relate to the user, to experiment with solutions to the problems that arise and, most importantly, to interact, to include the user in the process of producing their own health, making them subjects capable of creating autonomy in their way of going about life (FRANCO, 2007).

For this author, the dynamics of living labour in act bring the possibility of having the world of health in transformation and, above all, the implication of the subjects with the productive activity. All of this brings with it the power of change for workers and users (FRANCO, 2007).

Betting on the production of care where the work process of professionals is re-signified through the encounter of intersubjectivities is a possibility for confronting social inequalities and re-constructing the autonomy of subjects (PIRES;

DEMO, 2006).

In reality, thinking about integrality of care can mean incorporating the different needs of users and the context in which these health needs are produced into the production of health care and, in this way, reorganising the work processes between teams using the field of soft technologies.

CHAPTER 3

3. METHODOLOGICAL PATH

This is a qualitative study, as this approach makes it possible to understand the object being researched in its complexity (MINAYO, 2007). For this author, the qualitative approach answers very specific questions and has shown its contribution to the social sciences, particularly in the field of health, by working with the universe of meanings, motives, aspirations, beliefs, values and attitudes, corresponding to a deeper space of relationships that cannot be quantified.

Thus, this research was not concerned with quantification, but with understanding, through the methodological path of Oral History, the possible changes that occurred with ESF workers who took part in Community Therapy circles.

According to Bom Meihy (2007), Oral History can be defined as a practice of capturing narratives, one of the objectives of which is to produce documents that can be analysed, favouring studies of identity and collective memory. As a modern resource used for document production, archiving and studies relating to the social exposure of people and groups, it is always a history of the present time and is also known as living history.

Oral History has made new versions of history possible by giving voice to multiple and different narrators, as it has allowed this construction to be based on the words of those who experienced and participated in a given moment, according to their references and also their imagination. The presence of the past in people's immediate present is the raison d'être of oral history. The need for Oral History is based on the right to social participation, in other words, the right to citizenship itself (BOM MEIHY, 2007).

Oral history is an option for studying society through recordings of personal narratives, made from person to person, in which human relationships are valued. In this way, it enables new versions of history, based on the individual's narrative about the reality they experienced and pointing to society, grasping social relations in their entirety (BOM MEIHY, 2005, ROCHA, 2009).

According to Bom Meihy (2007), there are basically three types of Oral History: Life Oral History, Oral Tradition and Thematic Oral History. Oral Life History comprises a set of personal narratives about life experiences. Oral Tradition is the rarest and most complex category, working with the permanence and significance of myths, with the worldview of communities, which have values based on references to a distant past that are maintained through culture. And finally, Thematic Oral History is based on a specific previously established theme, committing itself to the clarification or opinion of the interviewee on a defined event, seeking the truth of those who witnessed an event or have a version of it that is debatable; in it, objectivity is direct.

Also according to Bom Meihy (2007), thematic oral history has a specific character and is very different from oral life history and oral tradition. Details of the narrator's personal history are only of interest insofar as they reveal useful aspects of the central thematic information. Not only does it allow the use of a semi-structured interview script with guiding questions, the so-called cut-off questions, but it is also a fundamental source for acquiring the details sought.

3.1. THE PLACE OF RESEARCH

The research was carried out in Health District II, located in the central-western region of João Pessoa-PB, which covers the neighbourhoods of Cristo, Rangel, Geisel, Grotão, João Paulo II, Funcionários II, III and IV, Colinas do Sul, Gramame, Loteamento Gervásio Maia and the Engenho Velho and Cuiá sites (JOÃO PESSOA, 2008).

Health District II was chosen as the setting for the research because in this district there have been several Community Therapy sessions involving different community groups and professionals from the various health occupations in the Family Health Strategy since the municipality introduced Community Therapy in 2007.

It is worth mentioning that the master's student worked in this district as a manager from January 2007 to January 2008, and during this time she had the opportunity to study Community Therapy, which helped her to conduct the wheels as a requirement of this qualification at the USFs in the district.

Health District II has a network of municipal health services with 38 Family Health Teams and a Comprehensive Health Care Centre (CAIS).

In terms of demographic characteristics, District II has an estimated population of 128,830 inhabitants. According to data from the Primary Care Information System (SIAB), 20,846 families are registered with primary care, totalling 119,562 people. Of these, 46.55 per cent are male and 53.45 per cent are female.

In the area of education, 96.8 per cent of children aged 7 to 14 are in school and 91.06 per cent of people aged 15 and over are literate (JOÃO PESSOA, 2008).

In terms of urban infrastructure, the vast majority of houses (98.28%) are made of brick, 99.71% of the water supply is through the public network, with filtered water in 48.5% of them, while 45.83% do not use any type of additional water treatment for consumption; 99.97% of properties have electricity; rubbish is disposed of in 98.04% of households by public collection; and faeces are disposed of in cesspits in 57.75% of them (JOÃO PESSOA, 2008).

The health services in this district are managed by a multi-professional matrix team, in which the supporter plays the role of health policy liaison and conflict mediator between the ESFs and the Health District. This supporter is responsible for making it possible for the ESFs to operate in line with the political project of the João Pessoa/PB SMS (JOÃO PESSOA, 2008).

3.2. STUDY COLLABORATORS

Of the Family Health Strategy workers who took part in the Community Therapy groups, eight professionals were chosen: 04 Community Health Agents, 01 Receptionist, 01 Dentist, 01 Nurse and 01 Doctor who are distributed across seven USFs in Health District II. Professionals who are not therapists, who have participated in at least four rounds of Community Therapy and who accepted the invitation to take part in the study were included.

In order to guarantee the anonymity of the collaborators in the study, their names were replaced by phenomena of nature in accordance with the discussion and combination held at the time of checking the material, with everyone agreeing to replace their name with a phenomenon of nature in accordance with Feng Shui and its location in the "ba-guá".

Feng Shui is an ancient Chinese science that has been practised for over 4,000 years. It studies the environment and the relationship between it and human beings, harmonising them. This ancient art is based on the idea that Chi energy is in all things in the physical world, giving life to the elements of nature in their different variations: colour, smell, taste and shape. This chi energy is carried by the currents of Feng (wind) and Shui (water), is in every space and has its own personality (SPALTER, H; STREICHER, 2000).

For the Chinese, when the space where you live or work is arranged with harmony, balance, common sense, creativity and intuition, life can be more balanced and harmonious, providing good health, prosperity, success, love, good relationships and spirituality. In ancient China, it was discovered that the world could be divided into five types of energy (elements) and they were given names from nature: fire, earth, metal, water and wood. These elements move inwards and outwards, ascend, descend and rotate (SPALTER, H; STREICHER, 2000).

According to Ventura (2008), the "ba-guá" is a kind of octagonal map used by Feng Shui to identify each of the corners (the guás) in the space where a person lives or works. The corners symbolise the areas of life: career, friends, creativity, relationships, success, prosperity, family, wisdom and health.

Each corner of the "ba-guá" is associated with a phenomenon of nature, in sequential order: 1-mountain, 2-water, 3-sky, 4-lake, 5-earth, 6-fire, 7-wind and 8-thunder, according to Spalter and Streicher (2000). In this way, the collaborators were distributed according to the sequence of the interviews, for example, the first collaborator interviewed corresponds to number (1), whose phenomenon of nature is the mountain, and so on. The meaning of each of these phenomena according to the aforementioned authors can be found in the next chapter of this study, in the construction of the opening window of the narrative of each story.

In this study, the option of using natural phenomena to guarantee the anonymity of the collaborators came up during the recording of the eighth interview, which took place in the garden of the collaborator's house. While listening to the narrative that was being recorded, the master's student was contemplating the natural setting in which they found themselves when she realised that she was completing eight interviews, which is the number of sides of the "ba-guá".

3.3. PRODUCTION OF EMPIRICAL MATERIAL

In order to produce the empirical material, a semi-structured interview script was used and notes were taken using the master's student's field notebook. According to Bom Meihy (2005), the field notebook records observations regarding the progress of the project, specific interviews and the researcher's impressions made throughout the process, becoming a reference for finalising the work.

The research collaborators were people who agreed to take part in the study. The selection of collaborators depends on the formation of a colony, defined by Bom Meihy (2007) as something that is exclusively linked to the foundation of the group's cultural identity; formed by the broad elements that confer the general identity of the segments willing to be analysed. Thus, the colony refers to the broad group, of which the network is the species or smaller part, in other words, the network is a subdivision of the colony and aims to draw up the inclusion/participation criteria for this study.

In this study, the colony was made up of professionals from the Family Health Strategy who have been taking part or have taken part in Community Therapy sessions since February 2007, and the network was made up of 8 professionals who have been taking part or have taken part in Community Therapy sessions for at least 4 Community Therapy sessions and have not studied Community Therapy.

Bom Meihy (2005) suggests that the central interview, which is richest in elements of the story in question, should be called "point zero". Point zero is understood to be a collaborator who knows the history of the group or person you want to interview centrally. After finding out what has been written about the case, one or more in-depth interviews should be carried out with this person, who is the custodian of the group's history or the reference for the history of other partners.

Once the network had been defined, the interviews were carried out in the following stages: pre-interview, interview and post-interview. These stages took place between September and December 2009. The "ground zero" interview, the one with Montanha, was considered to be a benchmark for significant changes in both the personal and professional dimensions of the employee and became a guide for the rest of the interviews.

The pre-interview corresponded to the first contact established with the collaborators, so that they were aware of the study, its objectives and the type of technique used to construct the empirical material, according to Bom Meihy (2007).

The interview itself was carried out at a time and place suggested by the collaborators, providing a calm and cosy atmosphere so that they could reveal their stories, which were recorded for later follow-up and archiving by the master's student and the institution.

According to Bom Meihy (2007), the interview needs to be guided by cut-off questions, defined as questions that permeate all the interviews and that must relate to the destination community, marking the identity of the group being analysed. With the collaborators' agreement to take part in the study, the cut-off questions that guided the interviews (Appendix C) were:

Have there been any changes in your personal life since taking part in the Community Therapy sessions?

What change(s) have occurred in your work process as a result of taking part in the Community Therapy circles?

Which change(s) do you consider to be the most significant?

After the interview, the recorded material was subjected to the three phases recommended by Bom Meihy (2005):

Transcription - at this point the material was transcribed in its entirety, with all the details contained in the interview;

Textualisation - the cut-off questions were removed and the text became narrative in nature. It was on this occasion that the vital tone of the interview was identified, i.e. the theme with the greatest expressive force within the collaborator's account was placed as the epigraph phrase in each narrative;

Transcribing - at this stage, the master's student interfered in the text, with a view to transcribing the textualised material, producing the final text to be taken to the collaborators for checking. At this point, the vital tone was defined by several readings of the material.

Then there was the post-interview, where each collaborator was thanked, the progress of the work was communicated, the process of constructing the text was explained and the meetings for checking it were scheduled.

Then, in previously arranged individual meetings, the text was presented by the master's student to the collaborators, and was checked, approved and authorised for use and publication in the study, by signing the Letter of Assignment (Appendix B), a document that defines this legality according to Bom Meihy (2005).

3.4. ANALYSING THE EMPIRICAL MATERIAL

The empirical material was analysed by identifying the vital tones of the interviews, which guided the construction of thematic axes based on the objectives

proposed in the research, and was guided by a process of discussion through a dialogue with the relevant literature.

Two thematic axes were thus constructed: Community therapy as a space that reveals learning, and Community therapy circles and the (re)signification of professional practices.

3.5. ETHICAL ASPECTS

As recommended by Ordinance 196/1996 of the National Health Council, which regulates research involving human beings, this study was sent to the Research Ethics Committee of the Lauro Wanderley University Hospital of the Federal University of Paraíba for analysis, where it was assessed and approved at a meeting on 25 August 2009, under protocol number 153/09, according to the copy of the certificate attached (Appendix A). Each collaborator signed the Free and Informed Consent Form (Appendix A), which deals with the objectives of the study and clarifies the rights of the collaborators, especially regarding the guarantee of anonymity, as well as the Letter of Assignment (Appendix B).

The Free and Informed Consent Form was completed in two copies, both labelled with the name of the participant and the Master's student, dated and signed, one of which was given to the research collaborator and the other kept by the Master's student (FRANCISCONI; GOLDIM, 2003).

The use of the texts was authorised by means of an assignment letter (Appendix B) which, according to Bom Meihy (2005), is a document that grants the author rights to use the interview, both the recording and the written result. Each collaborator checked the transcribed material by reading it individually in a reserved place previously scheduled for this occasion, according to their choice. At this point, it was also discussed and negotiated that their names would be replaced by fictitious names, guaranteeing their anonymity.

CHAPTER 4

4. TELLING STORIES

4.1. MOUNTAIN

"I've learnt to listen, because it's through listening that I can understand both myself and other people."

Mountain is the symbol of meditation. It symbolises climbing heights within ourselves to reflect on our experiences. When you feed "study and contemplation" with the seed of wisdom (knowledge) you grow. This is how this calm and attentive 34-year-old collaborator has turned out to be: she's married and the mother of a teenager. She lives in the community where she works, dedicating herself to her job as a Community Health Agent in an integrated Family Health Unit with three teams. She was very pleased to be invited to take part in the study and left it up to me to choose the time and place for our conversation, which took place very calmly over lunch on a day when she had scheduled time off in the afternoon:

I have noticed changes in my personal life as a result of my participation in the Community Therapy groups, and the most significant one is listening. I've learnt to listen, because it's through listening that I can understand both myself and other people, and then have a different way of helping. It's about listening and knowing how to deal with myself, so that I can put selfishness aside and share with others.

For me, putting listening first in my life was significant because in general we don't listen much because we think we don't have time, but we have time in life for everything, and Community Therapy also has a positive point in that being able to tell stories, both speaking and listening, being able to listen and listening is so important!

I only discovered that listening was important for me, for my personal development, in Community Therapy, and from then on I started listening to my husband at home, my son, my family and the people I work with, having my own time to listen, not just to the good things, but to the negative things too, because the good things are easy, what's good is good, it's ready-made and easy to deal with.

The most important thing is the bad because when you listen to what you don't want... What you don't like... What you don't like... That's where the conversation circle comes in, the exchange of experience. There in the Community Therapy circle I'm listening to this... I went through that... Or, I already know how I'm going to deal with that situation...

I can say: Community Therapy was a very good thing that happened in my life, I didn't know it happened in other places. Look, ever since I took part, when you say: "There's going to be therapy today"... Hail Mary! I get so anxious! "What time is it?" "When is it going to start?" I'd sit there and wait...

I can say that this work has brought a lot of gratification to the community! And as a Community Health Agent, Community Therapy has brought me another tool, another piece of work material, during home visits, on how to deal with families, with the problems I encounter on a daily basis, so Community Therapy for me is a key point, another learning experience in life and in my profession!

I learnt to love more, to understand more and to be more affectionate! Because, I imagine it like this: you give what you receive... So in Community Therapy it's a pleasant circle, there's that marvellous human warmth, you feel that affection, that welcome, that it's not an affection that you're giving out of obligation... It's not like that in Community Therapy. I feel that the therapist who leads the Community Therapy circle doesn't do it for the sake of doing it... She gives that human warmth, affection, cosiness, good feeling. Today I speak more softly, I speak more kindly to people, I'm more patient, I know how to listen to people more, how to hug, how to feel the other person!

I think the most significant change in my work is being able to help others, even with a hug or a smile, because just having someone to listen to me... The Therapist is a very important thing, when she leaves home, the instrument she takes with her is her heart... It's her ear... In the rodas, nobody knows what's going to happen at that moment, because there are people who have always been there, but there are new people... And they're new stories that bring different feelings and you're surprised all the time... In each circle that takes place, there are feelings that both feed the therapist's soul and our soul, because the person only has to come with body, soul and heart...

I think Community Therapy is marvellous, even more so than Psychotherapy, because sometimes a person is stuck in the psychologist's office and it takes several sessions for them to become uninhibited, whereas in a Community Therapy circle they feel free to talk about what's bothering them and they come out of a Community Therapy circle feeling great. I myself love Community Therapy because before I took part in the circles, I thought I was a super problematic person, I didn't know if it was me who had the world's faults or if it was the people around me who had the faults, but I had a doubt: if it was me who wanted to change people or if it was me who had to change in order to be able to work around or balance day-to-day life with these people.

So when I started to see other people's problems in the Community Therapy circles, that's when I realised that it was me who had to change, not other people. And as incredible as it may seem, today I live there in the Family Health Unit, even though it's a large unit with three Family Health Teams, but I live well because I learnt to change there!

I kiss the receptionist, the cleaner, the doctor, the nurse, I don't differentiate between people... Whoever doesn't like me, it's not my fault, but I give them the best of what I've learnt, and whoever doesn't want to give me anything in return is no longer my concern. Well, that's it, we expect the other person to change, but the other person never changes because first you have to know if the other person wants to change. That's how I put it!

Look, last week I was saying to my mum: "Look, mainha, in a fight between husband and wife, do you know why there's that saying that no one spoils anything? It's because you have to wait if the other person wants your opinion, you have to wait to find out if the other person wants your help. And he'll always give you a clue, when he's suffocating, he'll ask for help, he'll tell you."

"Come here, I'd like to talk to you"... But when you meddle in a couple's or family's life without asking, it doesn't work... Because when it comes to getting together, they don't ask for the family's opinion, they don't ask anyone's opinion, they get together on the sly, they choose themselves, or they choose too, when they come out to the family they've already chosen, they're in love and want to get married, and what do the parents do? They can't do anything. Now, when it comes to the problem... that's when the family has to come in? No. The two of them have to work it out together... If it was good to get them together in the beginning, it has to be good to destroy what's going wrong alone, and they can get back on their feet on their own, and if they need help... Ask.

4.2. WATER

"I learnt to listen, to respect, to take care of people as a whole [...] Of the mind and soul too [...] which is the most important thing."

It represents "deep water". For many of us, the biggest challenge in life is discovering and organising the work we would like to do. Being able to grow through her profession and carry out her work with enthusiasm is the fruit of learning in the life of this woman who, at 34, is cheerful and quiet, born in the hinterland of Paraíba, living in a comfortable house in the company of her husband and their two daughters. She works as a Community Health Agent with great enthusiasm and arranged for us to meet on a Sunday afternoon at her home, where I was able to enjoy a very cosy moment while the girls went to a birthday party and her husband watched a football match on television. We chatted quietly in the dining room of their home. Água takes part in the Neighbourhood Association's activities and is supporting initiatives related to the elderly group and the Family Health Unit, including promoting the discussion of Community Therapy as an activity to be revived for the community. I felt very welcome and was treated to a delicious homemade cake and coffee, kindly served by her, who was happy to talk about the effects of Community Therapy on her life and work, as she tells us below:

As a result of my participation in the Community Therapy groups, I believe that there has been a change in my personal life in terms of protection... Because I used to be overprotective of my daughters. I used to lock the girls up a lot, I wouldn't let them go there... As I once said in Community Therapy: They wanted to go for a swim in the pool and I wouldn't let them for fear! They cried a lot... And listening to people's stories in the Community Therapy circles, I learnt that I don't have the power to protect them all the time... I learnt to make them feel more at ease, that I can trust them a little and that I can let them play a little in the street, because I used to overprotect them... That's what I learnt in Community Therapy!

The most significant change in my personal life is what I said about the control I had over the girls... I've also learnt a lot as a health professional to listen to people as a whole, because sometimes a person just needs a word, to hear something...

With regard to the work process in the Family Health Strategy, before the Community Therapy groups, the team's relationship at work was very difficult because people were more individualistic and since the Community Therapy groups, there has been more affective contact and the relationship has improved between the professionals... We would arrive... Hugged... Smiled good morning! When Community Therapy stopped lately... The relationship is already a little frayed on the part of some members of the team, and there are some very difficult moments when we say this: Ah! I miss the Community Therapy sessions!...It's time we went back to the Therapies...

The Community Therapy circles were helping us a lot in our work because I believe that the circles create a better bond of affection? We stop!... You get to know the problem the other person is going through... Sometimes a person arrives at work "full" and we don't know why... Maybe it's because they're going through some problem at home and in the Community Therapy circle they get it out in the open, and the team, listening to their story, learns to respect them... That it's not because she's in a bad mood... It's because there's something behind it that's damaging it and in the CT session the team already knew... I know that the team's relationship got a little complicated after the therapy stopped, but I can say that we made a lot of progress with our participation in the Community Therapy sessions!

In my work process, the change that occurred was, as I said at the beginning, that I learnt to listen to people more, to look at people as a whole... Because before I used to count visits more as quantitative... I used to... I did... I did... And sometimes, when I arrived at a house... That person would start chatting... And because I had another visitor, sometimes I wouldn't even stay long enough... I'd run off to another one. Not today! After the therapy sessions, I learnt to listen more! I learnt that people don't always have illnesses that are physical illnesses and that we have to take care of ourselves, body, mind and soul! We have to listen!

When I arrive at a house where someone needs to talk, even though I know I have to make eight visits a day, but if I need to, I'll sit down and if the person stays there all morning talking, letting off steam... If I realise that they need it, I'll pay them a visit... But I listen... It's happened that I've arrived and thought my visit was going to be simple, because that family never had any problems and the lady was in great need... She was having a lot of difficulties with her husband, her marriage and all that confusion... It ended up that I spent most of the morning there listening...

I learnt in the Community Therapy sessions that we have to take care of the soul, and I think that just stopping, listening and letting off steam is significant, because when someone has a problem, sometimes what they want most is for someone else to stop and listen... And even at home, if you try to talk to someone who says: "Oh, I don't have time, you can talk to me later"... The person keeps it in and gets ill... As Community Therapy says, "when the mouth speaks, the organs are silent and when the mouth is silent, the organs speak"... That's exactly what I've learnt, and if the person is in need, I'll listen. My work process improved a lot after the Community Therapy sessions.

I can say that the most significant change for me is that of really listening to people and being able to help? There are even people who took part in the Community Therapy sessions who say that sometimes they arrived with a headache, sometimes they came very stressed and left without feeling anything else... They said: "It's like a holy remedy!"... One lady said: "I came here with a headache that I hadn't been able to stand when I started, I took part in the therapy circle, and in the end the headache was gone, the stress was gone"... Today, this lady who had a lot of problems with her marriage and had come to take part in the Community Therapy sessions, went to do Psychotherapy in another service where she could also talk because although Community Therapy isn't Psychotherapy, it helps a lot. Nowadays this lady has managed to completely change her life, in her marriage she got her husband to listen to her and see that they had a child with problems, and that it was getting worse because of the fights and disagreements in the house... And when her husband started fighting, she said: "Look, let's talk, because we have a child at home with problems and our fights are having a big impact", and that's how she said her life changed completely. Nowadays she's very much in control.

I consider the most significant changes to be: learning to listen, to respect, to take care of people as a whole... Of the mind and soul too, which is the most important thing! And here in my area, Community Therapy circles are very much needed because people are staying at home a lot without anyone to talk to or dialogue with... And they don't tell everyone on the street their problems because they have to have confidence... And in Community Therapy circles, the space gives this trust and the person taking part knows that what they say will be kept between the professionals who are there. It really helps!

4.3. HEAVEN

"Community Therapy helped me to accept the loss and today I can hear people talking about death and my heart no longer has that fear it used to have."

Heaven symbolises the power of the celestial forces from which all things come. It has the qualities of power, synchronisation, inspiration and confidence. When we align ourselves with good principles, they happen. Marks of benevolence are left on the path of our lives, helping us to fulfil our destiny when people and places give us inspiration and guide us. The sky is the principle of creativity that works through change, ensuring the proper order of all things: the sun shines, the rain falls and man progresses. The employee represented here is a cheerful and dynamic woman, aged 39, a nurse, married and the mother of a pre-teen son. She was very willing and happy to be invited to take part in this research and came to meet me late one afternoon after her daily eight-hour working day, but with a lot of energy and told me the following story in detail:

To begin with, I learnt about Community Therapy last year, in 2008, right? And I didn't know what it was... But from the first round of therapy I attended, I realised something quite different... It's not just a chat, it's something deeper, something more... And sometimes you even feel a bit out of place the first time... Personally, I found it very new, very different... You're there in a circle... Sometimes so big... Because the first time I took part, the circle was very big... And you feel so comfortable talking about your inner self, your innermost being, because often you're not telling secrets, you're telling feelings that involve your inner self... And you feel so comfortable talking, you know?

With my participation in the Community Therapy circles, I noticed changes from the first Therapy circle, because I thought something had changed, because I wanted to take part in others... I was keen to take part in other rounds... I didn't know when I'd get the chance... The first time I was a bit reserved because I didn't understand what was going on... So I wanted to get to know it first... I first wanted to know what it was all about, what the conversation was about and what it was going to lead to in the end, you know?

But I felt like taking part in other groups, and that was the first change, the desire to take part in other Community Therapy groups. Then came other opportunities, and I remember that the last Community Therapy session I took part in this year, which was in Health District II, I talked about my feelings, which in a way freed me up, because I felt very comfortable? There were lots of people talking about their feelings and that helped me to open up too... I talked about things that I don't usually get to talk about... Only to my best friends, you know? They weren't secrets, they were feelings...

I realise that today when I revisit the theme I spoke about in Therapy... To help other people... To really open my heart and receive help... Because in Community Therapy, we not only help, we also receive help... When we talk about an experience we've had, or that someone else has said and we've also had, we're not only helping that person, we're also helping ourselves... I felt that way!

So, the last Community Therapy session I attended was very important because I opened my heart to talk about things I never thought I'd talk about in a session, and it helped me a lot... Perhaps even to free myself from certain things that oppressed me, made me sad and made me an even unhappy person... I'll put it this way... So, when you take part in the Community Therapy circle and realise that other people suffer from feelings that you also suffer from, or that some people rejoice in certain things that you also rejoice in, you identify with them. This was very individual and very particular to my life.

And talking about the theme of Community Therapy, it's incredible when you stop and evaluate, because I'm evaluating something that I've never stopped to evaluate. And I can tell you that therapy really helps people to let go of things, to see the suffering of others, to stop being insensitive to certain things, to certain feelings that exist and sometimes you don't even give them any importance, you know? And it really did bring about changes in me.

I took part in about four Community Therapy Circles, including one that took place at the Changing Lives Family Health Unit, but the last one was the one that marked

me the most and brought about all those changes I've just mentioned... I can say that the most significant change was learning to deal differently with death. That was a one-off in my life and it was the fourth round of Community Therapy that helped me. Not that I learnt everything... But it gave me a much clearer vision, much more acceptable, much better. Because dying isn't bad for those who die, it's bad for those who stay alive, isn't it? And the last round of Community Therapy helped me a lot to accept the loss, because when I spoke in Therapy, I spoke about a loss, and until then I hadn't been dealing with this feeling very well, and it was the most important thing for me.
Community therapy that helped me...

Today I hear about loss, about death, and my heart no longer has the fear it used to feel... And look, I'm not young... And I'm not old, because I never will be! My spirit is young! But it's so good to learn! It's so good to be free of things! I think that this has been very good for me in therapy and if I continue to take part, other things will come and other lessons will be learnt! That's the most important thing in my personal life! To keep growing as a person!

And going from the personal side to the professional side, the Community Therapy circles helped because we started to think more about listening, listening to the other, because in the circle we listen a lot... You listen more than you talk... And together with other experiences I'm having in the Family Health Strategy here in João Pessoa-PB... Community Therapy has helped me with this, to have the patience to listen...

You're in a place that has a set start time and more or less a set finish time... And depending on the participants, it can take longer, can't it? I've learnt that you have to listen more carefully... And bringing this to the professional side: we're usually working and there's a start and finish time... There are a certain number of people waiting to be attended to, which is sometimes done very automatically and quickly because of time... And often the user wants to say something and you don't give them the chance to...

From my participation in the Community Therapy circles, I learnt that it is possible to listen, even with little time, and that you have to give quality to that time! You don't have to spend half an hour with a user to find out something or to hear from them something very important that they have to say, but take that minimum amount of time, and give quality to that time... And listening is important! You need to listen... And I don't know why people in the health sector don't listen much because I'm like that myself, I'm very keen to talk, to give advice, to listen, to talk about treatment... But with Community Therapy, I thought I was talking too much (laughs) and that I should talk less, you know?

This learning has helped me on a daily basis to put the user at ease... And so, when they arrive, they open their mouths and say what they want without me asking: "So, today, what do you want?", "What does he want?", "Why did you come?", "What's the reason for coming for a nursing appointment or to the Family Health Unit?" They say it themselves... I wait, I wait a minute or two and then they speak... And it was in the Community Therapy circles that I, as a health professional, learnt to listen.

In the work process, I took Community Therapy at first as something more individual and then I realised that I could bring it to the professional side. When there was a round of Community Therapy at the USF with the workers, I realised that, even though it was just one round, many people commented on how good it was, and also that they didn't like it, but among the people who did like it, I realised that there was a change too... To talk... That conversation the professionals have backstage: when are we going to drink water? Have a snack... Go to the toilet... I can say that Community Therapy helps professionals to relate to each other, to be together in a place like my unit, for example, where there are four Family Health Teams working together... That's a lot of people there... That's a lot of professionals working in that unit!

I think that Community Therapy has taught me this in my professional life: how to relate to others and also how to listen... You can associate this with welcoming, how to welcome people, because in Community Therapy you welcome so well... Everyone identifies themselves, says what they bring and in the end the person also says what they're taking away from Community Therapy, from that round of conversation, and welcoming is a conversation we have with the user.

These are things that we might think have nothing to do with it, but they do, because when you welcome someone well, you realise that they are disarmed, they are completely at ease with you, talking to you... And if you have a good reception with the user, they're more comfortable talking to you, to have an exchange with you, not just a health-disease exchange, but an individual, personal exchange, to talk about something personal, you know? If we don't manage to establish a rapport with the user, in other words, a good welcome, treating them with consideration, as if they really are a human being, worthy, and that the SUS is also worthy, you can't get them to feel a certain intimacy with you and it's just that technical professional/user relationship... It ended there, it died there... And I realise that Community Therapy taught me this too: to listen; when you arrive, to ask for the person's name, to call them by their name... You know that story when you're studying: "Mummy, push your child to be born", or, "Granny, where are you feeling pain?" And then we realise that it's not Granny, it's Dona Maria, or that the mother's name is Josefa... And... push for your child to be born, you know?

In Community Therapy circles, we learn that it's important for people to identify themselves and be treated as the human beings they are... The hug... That way of hugging... The way everyone hugs, sings and dances together breaks a tremendous ice in your life when you're taking part in a Community Therapy circle...

Bringing this to the work process, I realise that you also have to break the ice... The ice of indifference, the ice of the user thinking that they are wiser, or that they have more intelligence than them, or that they are more empowered by scientific knowledge and belittling the user, but they also have knowledge... They also have knowledge about herbs, teas and things that they know, but which is sometimes underestimated or looked down upon...

So I think that Community Therapy... My God in heaven... It's done so many things! It's about treating others as human beings, as you would like to be treated... Because I'm also a SUS user, and when I go for an appointment I find it beautiful and marvellous when the person treats me well... I feel good, it's like I'm not even a nurse, I'm just someone from the community providing that service.

Lately, I've needed SUS a lot, both for myself and for my son, and I even praised it when I went to the Jaguaribe CAIS (I can say these things, can I?). I went to the Jaguaribe CAIS and I thought it was so organised, everything was so beautiful, everything was so organised, with the most human people... I went straight to the nursing room, where I was asked a few questions, then had my blood pressure checked, then measured and weighed...

I said:

"Guys, how good is this business here!"

And they asked me:

"How long have you been here?"

I replied that it had been almost a year and went on to say that the reception room there was beautiful, clean, organised, with a glass desk and air conditioning, and that the work there had changed a lot:

"Your work here is very good!"

When I said:

If only the PSF had a desk like that and air conditioning! Your work is very good! That's when they asked me where I worked, and I replied that it was at the Family Health Unit, and that, for the time being, the room doesn't have air conditioning, but it has a very good atmosphere! I mentioned this here because people often don't realise what they have... For example, I thought my environment was great, because my room is big, and although there's no air conditioning, there's a window that ventilates... But when I got to CAIS (laughs)... With everyone working with air conditioning... I complimented them, and as a SUS user, I found the way I was treated very interesting, and I told them so:

You're treating me well, I'm enjoying seeing you, and even though I didn't know if you were a nurse or a nurse technician, you've looked after me well, you've welcomed me well...

I associated this experience with the user at the PSF, and I thought: "My God! Am I being welcoming in this way?" And this also encouraged me to see myself as a provider, I don't know if I can put it like that... I'm a health producer... I produce health... And I'm also a user, and I receive guidance for my health, you know?

In other places where I've experienced a certain delay, I've felt the same way as the other person at the PSF, who spends two hours waiting to be seen... That's when you feel like a user too... It's very good to put yourself in the other person's shoes, and you know how to respond when they're agitated, complaining:

"Ah! I have to pick up my boy from school!"

"Ah! I have to get the bread!"

"I have to get my milk!"

And we often don't understand... And sometimes we give a rude answer, you know? And when we're users, we give an answer like this: "Look, the doctor inside hasn't stopped working, he's in there attending, let's be patient"... I'm working on my patience at CAIS... And in the afternoon I went there for a test and I couldn't work because I'd spent the whole afternoon there... That's when you feel like a user and you have to become more human to understand the other side too... It really is stressful working with human beings because everyone has their own way of being and reacting, as in all relationships... And when you go through both roles, as a SUS worker and as a user too, you understand, and today I fully understand the user who is stressed!

With regard to the most significant changes, I can say that listening is very significant... In the Community Therapy circle, we learn to listen, because you can't talk to anyone while the other person is talking (which is one of the rules of therapy). ...And humanisation!.. I think that when you listen, you're already treating with humanisation, and it's already a way of valuing the other person, because when you cut them off, you're devaluing them... You learn to contain yourself!

So the Community Therapy circles help you to listen, to treat people humanely, even to hug someone you've never seen before, because there are always new people at work. One thing I always do before entering my office is to say good morning to everyone, and when there are elderly people or people who are more receptive, I take their hand... And I see that the others start to raise their hands too... And I go over there, saying good morning, taking their hand... Even holding hands is an ice-breaker... And the hug is even bigger.

Generally, we don't get to the point of embracing... But there are some elderly users that the team accompanies in the locality... That we hug... Because we don't have a lot of time to hug people, but there are certain moments that are important... And in therapy we learn that... to hug! And that breaks the ice even more... It puts the user at ease and makes the relationship much more bonding!

I'm with someone in my area who was depressed and since starting a group at her house she's changed and has already told me how important it's been for her life.

I can tell you that when you take part in the Community Therapy circles, you realise that it's good to hug... To listen... That it's good to give importance to what people have to say... Then we bring this into our personal and professional lives. So, basically, those are the changes!

4.4. LAKE

"Trying to listen to your neighbour and looking at the human being as a whole [...] wherever you are, having that look..."

The lake symbolises a vast expanse of calm waters, which represent the joy of happiness. It is associated with the qualities of pleasure, generosity and encouragement. By positively stimulating other people, we bring pleasure and success to ourselves. This is the central idea of this teaching. We need to give in order to receive, it's the law of life. Generosity is a characteristic of this employee, a young, caring and determined woman. She is 29 years old, married and has two daughters. She works as a receptionist in a Family Health Unit with four Family Health Teams and has lived in the same neighbourhood since she was born. Our conversation took place at the end of a working day in one of the rooms at Valentina Municipal Hospital, thanks to her generosity in arranging the interview for my workplace. She told me the following story calmly and without fear of expressing herself:

From my participation in the Community Therapy circles, I realised a change in my personal life, yes? When I told you about my husband's drug use... That was very difficult for me and the most significant change was this... It was very difficult for me... I didn't know how to resolve the various situations that had been happening, such as when he came round and wanted to sell things from inside the house to exchange for drugs and we'd get into fights... Sometimes he wanted to sell the jerry can, and I wouldn't let him because we have children... I'd look for a solution... Sometimes I took a breath... And I couldn't find the best way out... Because he wouldn't listen to me... And in the Community Therapy circle, I had the opportunity to meet people I didn't even know... Who I least expected, but who were there listening to me and trying to understand me as best they could.

And as a health professional, I've realised that Community Therapy is very significant in the work process in the Family Health Strategy and that it's worth taking part because through Community Therapy you can find ways of working better... For example, when you often can't understand why the user arrives so aggressive... And you often don't understand... And through CT you understand why that person is so aggressive that they even want to attack you... And you'll only understand when you're in a Community Therapy circle, where that anguish comes from? Where that suffering comes from... All that upset...

From my participation in the Community Therapy circles, in my work process, change was inevitable because I began to realise when I tried to put myself in the user's shoes... how difficult it is... How difficult it is... Would I want to arrive at a Family Health Unit and be told no straight away?... Through Community Therapy, I realise that a fundamental part of this whole story has also been in relation to welcoming, trying to listen to others, putting yourself in their shoes as you would like to be welcomed... And so I've learnt a lot.

The most significant change that I consider is having a view of the human being as a whole, and not just at that moment, but at various moments, wherever you are, having this view and this flexibility, being flexible especially when you are in contact with the user, with the professional and with the agendas relating to the work process.

I still take part in the Community Therapy sessions whenever I can, because they take place at the USF on Thursday afternoons with the Doctor and there is also one with a Community Health Agent at a church in the community. And I can say that it's productive work because many people, especially those who use psychotropic drugs and don't accept it because it's a drug and everyday life has made them use it, can also benefit from the Community Therapy sessions.

One day there was a patient who cried at the Family Health Unit because she said she couldn't live without Rivotril[1] , and the other day I said to her: Look lady, here's the deal: every Thursday there's Community Therapy, why don't you come and join in? And I invited her, who was crying a lot, distressed and saying that she couldn't live without Rivotril, and I told her that that was a drug and she didn't need to be using that drug to live, to feel better? And that there are other ways for people to survive, and that Community Therapy teaches a lot, because it taught me, it's where I learnt how to live better, how to avoid some difficult situations, how to really face the truth, how to face the barriers, the difficulties and the hurdles of life.

The Community Therapy circles help a lot because there you have the opportunity to listen to people, to put yourself in the other person's shoes, and that's very gratifying. This lady hasn't had the opportunity yet, but I told her that my life has changed a lot both personally and professionally since I took part.

4.5. LAND

"I became calmer, more patient, listening more to the users and also to the whole team."

Earth symbolises earthly forces. It is associated with adaptability, devotion and conditional support, qualities found in true love and happy marriages. These characteristics epitomise this calm and persevering collaborator, 66 years old, a doctor, married, very devoted to his family and who demonstrated his special relationship with his grandson in the Community Therapy sessions. He is a practising Catholic and takes part in a church congregation. He cultivates long-lasting friendships, leaving strong bonds wherever he goes, as witnessed by the tribute he received at Christmas 2008 from the members of the Family Health Team he had previously been part of. He was very willing to take part in this study and chose the Family Health Unit where he is a team doctor as the location for the interview, and with great lightness and objectivity he revealed the following narrative:

From my participation in the Community Therapy circles, I realised that generally the person who takes part in the first CT circle already feels lighter, calmer, more patient and more secure. Because often the person comes to work and is afraid, impatient, agitated... I felt calmer, with more objective work.

That's why I think my participation in the Community Therapy circles was very important! And its consequences are still very important! The most significant change

[1] Rivotril - the name of a psychotropic drug (which requires a special prescription).

I've noticed is the peace of mind I've acquired in my work and today I try to attend more calmly and patiently, listening more to the users.

Community Therapy is important in any case, especially in the work of the Family Health Unit, where we deal with all kinds of people, especially people with little schooling, and if you don't have a certain tranquillity, and a certain patience? which I acquired in the Community Therapy circles... If you don't, you live in a constant war of nerves, because one wants one thing and the other wants another... And we have to conduct our work in a way that reassures the users.

As soon as I took part in the Community Therapy sessions, I became calmer, more patient, I listened more to the users and also to the whole team... Which is very important... And in the team, as the backbone of the community in which it operates, I feel I've had a change in the way I work... The way I practice my profession... The way I look after users... Home visits, because they're tiring... Especially here, where there are lots of hills... We go up and down hills... And you deal with people from all walks of life... And you have to adapt or make the user adapt to you as well, and that's why I say that the most important thing I've acquired is precisely that, patience to deal with these situations and to practise.

After the Community Therapy sessions, I was calmer and even slept better, I'm sleeping, with work, tiredness, the stress of everyday life, and after the Community Therapy sessions that's it. It's very important and I miss it!

"I learnt to value listening and hearing what the other person wants and feels."

Fire symbolises a bright flame that rises like two torches, illuminating and refining the world. Friendly relationships emerge around it when it cultivates a good reputation, favouring better chances for a peaceful and secure future. This flame seems to illuminate this collaborator, who has always been very willing to take part in Community Therapy sessions and always radiates a lot of light with his presence. He is a young man, very attentive, 29 years old, has a degree in Dentistry and is studying for a post-graduate qualification in Family Health. He is an active participant in the Community Therapy groups and is very willing to collaborate, both with testimonies and with aggregation rituals. When he was invited to take part in this study, he was very willing and suggested we talk at the headquarters of Health District II, which took place at the end of a quiet morning after he had attended to the users, and he told the following story:

As a result of my participation in the Community Therapy circles, I have certainly noticed a change in my personal life, because in the rush of life, in everyday life, we realise that we stop listening to people. You stop sitting down and taking the time to listen to their life experiences or their problems. There are the difficulties faced by health professionals who always want to medicalise all of people's pains and often forget that a simple attitude of listening, and hearing what the other person wants and feels, already brings about a great transformation for the person speaking, and this has changed the way I look at people.

In addition to the changes I've listed, I realised that, especially after the Community Therapy circles and even during the process itself, I felt very well. When you also put yourself as a patient in that circle, and we're all the same, we forget a little about the professional side and become co-participants, like everyone else there... And when we really expose ourselves, when we put ourselves into this wheel experimentation, we see how it works, how it works... So this thing about "when the mouth is silent, the organs speak", and "when the mouth speaks, the organs heal", is something really scientifically proven, because I've seen it in myself and I've seen in those people the transformation, especially emotional, of well-being.

In my work process, I realise that the biggest influence is valuing listening to people, people in a hurry: "What now? Are we going to medicate straight away?" No. That was already a

It's been a habit of mine to try to listen, but I've really valued what people have said even more, not just me but all the professionals who are part of the Family Health Team... We really try to sit down, listen, really let people talk... And there are consultations that used to last five minutes and now last fifteen or twenty... Just the person sitting, talking... That's what happened today. I spent more than twenty minutes with someone chatting before coming for the interview, and it's really gratifying because the person is reassured and more confident about what has been proposed for them as therapy.

The changes that I consider most significant, apart from this attitude, are the results that I see on a daily basis, in the practice of exercising... Because Community Therapy has brought me, as a health professional, another proposal for care that isn't just for that moment in the circles and you forget about it... It brings learning to yourself and if you see that it's something good, you have to share it with others, and my way of sharing... The lightness I felt... It breaks the heart that gets really tight from all the pain it hears...

So I feel that in my daily practice, the increase in listening time has brought more confidence to the users and more receptiveness to the therapy and certainly more lightness in the approach to them... I always see it as positive, and so far I haven't seen any side effects from the Community Therapy Circles. Honestly, it's really changed, and if we dedicate ourselves a little bit and are really willing to change, it's not just good for us, it's good for others too!

"I've learnt to be more patient and listen first, then speak my mind [...]"

Wind symbolises softness. You adopt qualities of patience, trust and balance, building a solid financial base. Reward and happiness come from having friends, family and good health. Living by this principle means taking care of the people, places and things that bring abundance and prosperity into our lives. The employee represented by this element seems to associate these characteristics and is showing his evolution as a person and as a health professional every day. He is 37 years old, married and has a daughter to whom he always refers with great dedication. He works as a Community Health Agent with great commitment and was delighted to receive the invitation to collaborate in this research, scheduling our conversation to take place at the Family Health Unit where he works, which happened in an atmosphere of great trust and spontaneity, as shown in his narrative:

From my participation in the Community Therapy circles, I certainly realised that my personal life changed for the better, because I learned a new way of looking at those around me, a way of acting, and it was through the Community Therapy circles, listening, because in Community Therapy no one gives advice to anyone, but exchanges experience? I took this home with me... And it's still working today, thank God!

The most significant change I realise, I believe, is patience... I think I used to be very impatient with those around me, even with my own daughter... I've learnt to be more patient and to listen first and then speak my mind... I say that patience is of fundamental importance to me because I'm having more patience with the people who live with me in my house.

I can say that in relation to Community Therapy in the work process in the Family Health Strategy, that before the Therapy circles here in our Health Unit, it was different because if we came in and said good morning and the other person didn't respond, we didn't know why... And sometimes I ignored why that person was in a bad mood because I can act one way and that person can't... They might be going through a season of life and I might not understand... And in the Community Therapy circles I learnt not to giving advice and trying not to invade other people's lives... I could even exchange experience...

I was given the opportunity to share my experience, to pass on something, which I took to Therapy itself and here to the team was of fundamental importance, because nowadays I can look at a person and say: "I'm not going to criticise them because they must be going through some problem". And before I say anything, I first observe and wait for the next day... Sometimes this happens a lot here and the next day the person comes back a different person... A season of life that she was going through that if I had hit her head on I would have totally missed her new season, autumn, summer, you know? I've learnt to observe that now...

I'm not an easy person, but both my participation in the Community Therapy circles has taught others to understand me and me to understand others, I've understood this way, in this way, and thank God we're dealing with it, I myself have learnt... I'm not going to say I'm 100 per cent... But I've drawn from some of the experiences I've heard and witnessed in Community Therapy circles, and I've learnt to live with it, and to take it literally, and thank God everything is working out! In my work process, my main change I think has been to be more participative, because I think I was still very individualistic... And I've learnt to be more participative with my work colleagues... Because I believe that within the workplace, even if it's a team, there's still that individuality, right? I learnt that, and I like to participate, I like to help, you know? And I passed this on in the Community Therapy circles, without giving advice, I said my experience, what I was going through, what I felt, and I carry that with me. I like taking part - I can tell you that if you talk to any of my work colleagues here, they know what I'm like... I like everyone, I understand other people's sides, I've come to understand other people's sides better! Firstly, I wanted to say the following: Community Therapy, I see it like this: in our lives I compare it to a wardrobe, when we don't talk, don't let off steam, it's like a wardrobe, we keep accumulating things, like in a suitcase, which keeps accumulating, accumulating, accumulating, and then there comes a time when it collapses on top of us.In Community Therapy circles there's the opportunity to let off steam, to contribute, for someone to identify with someone else's problem, to pass something on to you, for you to be able to react, you know? Because I can go through a problem and not know how to solve it, but in a Community Therapy circle, a person with the same problem as mine may have done well, and I'll exchange that experience, they'll pass it on to me, not in the form of advice, but as an experience and I'll follow it, if I want to. So I think that our life, in my view, is like a suitcase that we accumulate, accumulate, then there comes a time when we want to get it off our chest, then we throw it all at whoever it hurts, whoever is in front of us... So this made me reflect a little and the Community Therapy sessions encouraged me a lot, helped me a lot not to let go of what I have in terms of anguish, so that I don't throw it at others, that others have nothing to do with what I'm going through, okay?I think that's what's helped me, I believe I've changed, the change has been for the better, I believe for the better because if you talk about it, not just with me, but with everyone on the team, everyone has changed for the better, I don't think we've regressed, we haven't regressed, we've progressed for the better.I think one of the best changes that came from those meetings was the realisation, as I've already said in all these previous questions here: "why is so-and-so doing this?", "why is so-and-so doing that?" we're not putting anyone up against the wall, that this isn't good, and we're not dictating rules!

I think the important thing in the group is to seek partnerships and companionship and we're achieving that, because everyone is already a professional, because if they weren't they wouldn't be working where they are... More companionship, more dedication and more commitment is what everyone has here today in this Health Unit. And before the Community Therapy circles there were times of turbulence when nobody understood anybody. We'd get here, we'd kick down each other's doors, you know? If I came with a problem from home and the person looked at me crossly, I wanted to take it out on them, and I'd take it out on others too, and since the Community Therapy sessions, we've moved on, thank God! I have this different outlook now, I don't hit anyone anymore, as a first step I count to ten, and I see what I'm going to say to this person, if this person really deserves to hear what I'm going to say? Is what I'm about to say to them fair? So those were the changes here in the team, and I liked them... And on home visits, you have to think about everything, because I see my visitors as members of my family because you get closer, you create a bond, and I've learnt to see people with different eyes. There's even someone I won't name, a user in my micro-area who I used to get very annoyed with, because she would come in and practically shout when she came into the health unit... And once I went to her house to carry out a home visit and she said: "You're not coming in here because you treat me badly where you work at the health centre." And I spoke to her and said: "Look, let me in because I want to talk to you, I want to understand why you're angry"... And after insisting for so long, she let me in... And so I realised that she's a woman on her own, you see? She doesn't have anyone to talk to... The people closest to her have done her the favour of abandoning her... So sometimes when she comes here to the Family Health Unit, it's to let off steam... I tried to understand this lady and nowadays when she comes, I know how to deal with her... If she comes with seven stones in her hand and I go in with eight, it won't do any good. So I have to let my guard down... Sometimes a touch on the shoulder, a more affectionate treatment of this lady... And there are so many other cases... But thank God I managed to deal with this lady and get over it... And the atmosphere at work and during my visits is much better, because I've taken it into my visits too! It's much better! Now I can see a person not by what they're saying, but let's see what they're going through and why they're like that? And the Community Therapy sessions have been important for the user I'm visiting, because I've gained experience in dealing with this, I've learnt not to advise anyone, and there are people who don't like advice, but I've learnt to tell them a story, I say: "Look, I'm going to tell you a story that's more or less identical to yours, you know?" And so I talk, I tell them how I was. And so I tell them, I tell them how I got on and I leave it up to them to choose... And that's how I sometimes succeed with this user.

So it was great! It was very worthwhile to take part in the Community Therapy sessions. It was of great value to me!

4.8 TROUBLE

"I feel more human and I realise that the team has come closer to the community"...

Thunder symbolises movement and power, expressing the need to cultivate physical health, emphasising the importance of patience in relation to love with the family to act as a support in difficult phases of life. Well structured, it favours expansion, growth and happiness in life. In this way, this employee seems to embrace nature and bring it close to him and his family. He is 66 years old and lives with his wife and a daughter in a condominium near the Family Health Unit where he is a Community Health Agent. He's very studious in various areas, but it's phytotherapy that he's particularly identified with, and he even enjoys beautiful specimens of live drugs in the garden and backyard of his house in perfect harmony with other ornamental and fruit-bearing plants that have been carefully planted. Our conversation took place on the terrace of this pleasant residence, with a snack that he had prepared himself and a delicious coffee to accompany this narrative:

As a result of my participation in the Community Therapy sessions, I've noticed some changes in my personal life, yes, because I feel more like a family with the team, and with some of the users who took part, there's been a much closer relationship and this has led to a great enrichment in the work process. I liked it a lot and we're asking to come back because there really is a lot of personal growth with Community Therapy. I believe that the most significant change is this question of feeling more human. Community Therapy leads to a very humanising process and since I believe that the work process only moves forward when there is humanisation, then the most significant change was precisely this issue of humanisation, not only for me, but also in my relationship with my work colleagues, with the whole team.Although there was this very large window without the practice of Community Therapy, I saw that there was growth, as I said before. I even see people from the community who took part asking when Community Therapy is coming back. I realise that the team got closer to the community, even though there was little contact... If it had continued, today the team would be way ahead, much closer to the community, because Community Therapy in this process of humanisation brings the community closer to the unit and the unit closer to the community because we notice that sometimes the community wants to get closer, but the unit distances itself, and Community Therapy has played such an important role for the Family Health Unit in this rapprochement, even though there hasn't been massive community participation.From my participation in the Community Therapy circles, I can say that the first change in my work process was, as I've already said, from the humanisation, there was a rapprochement with the team, a greater understanding with others and, consequently, a broader vision to understand the work of others, and hence there was this integration in the work process.The changes that I consider to be the most significant are the team's closeness and unity, truly forming a team, because it goes from a group to a team, and as I said earlier, if the Community Therapy sessions had continued, there would certainly have been a lot more of a team, there would have been a lot more growth and, consequently, the work would have gone much better. I think we have a thirst for Community Therapy. Even some members of the team who had a certain resistance, now also feel this gap and I felt that these people who had more resistance, have already opened up and revealed the need for Community Therapy. And I found this very interesting: people who used to stay on the sidelines have already said that there has been real growth since the Community Therapy sessions.

CHAPTER 5

5. DISCUSSING THE EMPIRICAL MATERIAL: REVEALING LEARNINGS AND CHANGES

The fragments of these stories are significant for a better understanding of their experiences, from which two thematic axes were constructed: **Community Therapy as a space that reveals learning, and Community Therapy wheels and the (re)signification of professional practices.**

5.1.. COMMUNITY THERAPY AS A SPACE FOR LEARNING

According to Barreto (2008), during the process of participating in Community Therapy circles, users have the opportunity to re-signify their life stories and rebuild a new identity, without opening up a solution of continuity in their history.

In trying to understand what happened to the ESF professionals as a result of their experience in the Community Therapy circles, learning was identified as a significant change in the reports of the collaborators in this study.

Learning to listen precedes any form of learning, and so it is worth recalling the influence of the pedagogical approach of Community Therapy, as Barreto (2008) states that Community Therapy, as a space for promoting interpersonal and inter-community encounters, aims to value the participants' life stories, recover identity, restore self-esteem and self-confidence, broaden the perception of problems and the possibilities of finding options for resolving problem situations as a result of the learning process experienced collectively. In this sense, the collaborators reveal:

> [...] I learnt to listen, because it's through listening that I can understand both myself and other people, and then have a different way of helping. It's about listening and knowing how to deal with myself so that I can put my selfishness aside and share with others (Montanha).
>
> [...] I learnt a new way of looking at the people next to me, a way of acting, and it was through the Community Therapy circles, listening, because in Community Therapy nobody gives advice to anyone, but they exchange experiences [...] I took this home with me (Vento).
>
> [...] I think there has been a change in my personal life in terms of protection [...] Because I used to be overprotective of my daughters [...] I used to lock the girls up a lot, I wouldn't let them go out there [...] I learnt that I don't have the power to protect them all the time [...] (Água).

For Guimarães (2006), identifying changes in the lives of participants in Community Therapy groups is of great value, making it possible to affirm that Community Therapy, as a technology of care, has contributed to improving people's quality of life based on the reflections generated during the meetings.

According to Barreto (2008), Community Therapy provides opportunities to share suffering in which expressing oneself without fear of being judged, giving visibility to the pain, makes it possible to re-signify this suffering and transform it into stories of overcoming, becoming a resilient being.

According to Pinheiro (2004), resilience is a challenge of the millennium in a modern society in which changes are increasingly rapid and profound, requiring constant adaptation. In this way, this research was able to identify examples of resilience promoted through Community Therapy circles in the following accounts:

> [...] I can say that the most significant change was learning to deal with death in a certain way [...] It gave me a much clearer vision, much more acceptable, much better [...] It helped me a lot to accept loss [...] Today I hear about loss, about death, and my heart no longer has that fear it had before [...] (Céu).
>
> [...] I didn't know how to resolve the various situations that were happening [...] that's where I learnt how to live better, how to avoid some difficult situations, how to really face the truth, how to face the barriers, difficulties and obstacles of life (Lago).
>
> [...] I realised that generally the person who takes part in the first round of Community Therapy feels lighter, calmer, more patient, more secure. Because often the person comes to work and is afraid, impatient, agitated [...] I felt calmer, with more objective work (Terra).

According to Carmelo (2006), people are able to adapt and overcome difficult situations when they reflect on their experiences, demonstrate their competences, such as self-confidence, self-esteem and clarity of purpose, and if they accept possible changes more easily.

According to Leal (2007), in order to believe in change, it is necessary to be sensitive and understand that there is a conduct in each question that leads to reflection, to thinking that drives the search for theoretical and practical references, thus promoting genuine and participatory existential dialogue. From this comes a magical moment that occurs in the alchemy of encounter, of transformation, with listening as the basic element, because any listening requires emptying oneself of values and meanings in order to develop a loving relationship with oneself and with others.

In the narratives recorded, the collaborators express that they have noticed changes in their lives and highlight the importance of learning to listen, referring to the appreciation of listening as a significant change and that this discovery has contributed to modifying personal, family and professional relationships, since they felt sensitised by the stories of shared experiences, as revealed in the following statements:

> I only discovered that listening is important for me, for my personal development, in Community Therapy, and from then on I started listening to my husband at home, my son, my family and the people I work with [...] Having my own time to listen, not just to the good things, but to the negative things too [...] (Montanha).
>
> The Community Therapy circles helped because we start to think more about listening, listening to others, because in the circle we listen a lot [...] We listen more than we speak [...] Community Therapy helped me with this, to have the patience to listen [...] (Céu).
>
> [...] You learn something for yourself and, if you see that it's good, you have to share it with others, and that's my way of sharing [...] The lightness that I felt [...] It breaks the heart that gets really tight from all the pain you hear [...] (Fogo).
>
> [...] I've noticed a change in my personal life, yes, because I feel more like a family with the team, and with some of the users who took part there was a much closer relationship and this has led to a great enrichment in the work process (Trovão).

According to Barreto (2005), as people talk about their suffering and say what they have done to resolve it, an attempt is made to highlight the strategies used by each individual. We discover that where there has been suffering, knowledge has been built up that has enabled it to be overcome. It cannot be denied that individuals and social groups have their own mechanisms for overcoming adversity. The socialisation of this knowledge generates a dynamic movement between the *vertical* reading of oneself and the *horizontal* reading with others. By listening to the other person's experience, each person refers to their own, allowing them to make discoveries, become aware and discover that each person has their own trajectory and produces their own knowledge.

Community Therapy, anchored in Freire's Pedagogy (2005), proposes the horizontality of the relationships between the components of group work as a path towards the transformation of each person and the world in a call to action and reflection based on the exchange of experiences. In this research, the influence of this statement can be seen in the reports that say:

> So when I started to see other people's problems, other people's faults, in the Community Therapy sessions, that's when I realised that it was me who had to change, not other people (Montanha).
>
> [...] I did notice a change in my personal life. When I told you about my husband's drug use [...] That was very difficult for me and the most significant change was that [...] It was very difficult for me (Lago).
>
> [...] I've learnt to be more patient and to listen first, and then speak my mind [...] I say that patience is of fundamental importance to me because I'm having more patience with the people who live with me in my house (Vento).
>
> I can say that the most significant change for me is that of really listening to people and being able to help [...] (Water).

For Grandesso (2005), the network of conversations that takes place in Community Therapy is organised by the meanings constructed around human suffering and constitutes a context in which each person can be recognised as a legitimate human being, regardless of their origin and circumstances.

According to Rocha (2009), in Community Therapy each user is seen as a being full of knowledge and feelings, which makes it possible to develop an open and reflective dialogue, thus leading participants to interact and exchange knowledge within their own reality.

According to Barreto (2008), community therapy circles create a space for participants to speak, which is therapeutic for both the speaker and the listener, in the sense of providing learning through the sharing of experiences.

The attitude of respect towards the content of their speeches and their feelings; the valuing of the life experience of Community Therapy participants provides an atmosphere of acceptance and affection. In this way, participants feel free and confident to share their feelings without the risk of being judged or excluded (SOARES, 2008). The statements below exemplify this statement:

> [...] I felt like taking part in other groups, and that was the first change, the desire to take part in other Community Therapy groups [...] I spoke about my feelings, which in a way freed me, because I felt very comfortable [...] There were a lot of people talking about their feelings and that helped me to open up too [...] I spoke about things that I usually can't talk about [...] (Céu).
>
> [...] And in the Community Therapy circle, I had the opportunity to have people I didn't even know [...] who I least expected, but who were there listening to me and trying to understand me in the best possible way (Lago).
>
> [...] I've certainly noticed a change in my personal life, because with the hustle and bustle of life, on a daily basis, we realise that we stop

> listening to people. You stop sitting down and taking the time to listen to their life experiences or their problems (Fogo).
>
> [...] And through the Community Therapy circles I learnt not to give advice and try not to invade other people's lives, you know? [...] I could even exchange experiences... (Vento).

According to Barreto (2008), there are several paths that lead to knowledge and confer competence on those who walk them. The great road to professional training has been the institutions that hold knowledge and another source of knowledge is personal experience throughout the lives of individuals and social groups. The difficulties overcome are transformed into sensitivity and competence to face other sufferings.

This knowledge, built on the need that generates competence, makes it possible to affirm that by caring for others, everyone is caring for themselves, because in this way, by caring for others, they are restoring their own personal and family history.

Barreto (2008) also states that a word, a gesture of support can make a difference between those who fail and those who win and, in Community Therapy, as people share their suffering, they transform their feelings and enable a re-signification of traumatic events, weaving social bonds and generating a sense of belonging to the group.

In this study, the employees revealed significant changes in their lives and feelings of well-being, as can be seen in the following narratives:

> After taking part in the Community Therapy sessions, I became calmer, more patient, I listened more to the users and also to the whole team [...] (Terra).
>
> [...] After the Community Therapy circles and even during the process itself, I felt very comfortable, when the person also sees themselves as a patient, who is in that circle and we are all the same, we forget a little about the professional side and we become co-participants like everyone else there (Fogo).
>
> The most significant change I realise, I believe, is patience... I think I used to be very impatient with those around me, even with my own daughter (Vento).

According to Guimarães (2006), in modern society, due to the fast pace at which people live, there is no time to talk about their anxieties, fears, disappointments and sadness, and so they transfer symptoms such as back pain, gastritis, depression and even neoplasms to the physical body as a way of demonstrating the emotional or social suffering they experience.

According to Cairo (1999), the body is the canvas on which emotions are projected and, according to this author, negative emotions are projected through illnesses, and these somatisations will occur in the short or long term. Unhappiness, grief, anger, hurt and resentment are feelings that, when stored for a long time, will lead to the most serious illnesses.

In Community Therapy circles, participants are encouraged to express their emotions and feelings, releasing the tensions resulting from stress. Barreto (2008) says that it's common to remember, at the beginning of the groups, the popular saying: "when the mouth is silent, the organs speak and when the mouth speaks, the organs heal". They are encouraged to speak with their mouths so as not to talk about depression, insomnia, gastritis or other illnesses. In this way, the employees recognise the importance of being able to count on a space to speak and listen in their lives, as the following statements indicate:

> [...] And when we really expose ourselves, when we put ourselves into this experimentation of the wheel, we see how it works, how it works,

> because I have seen in myself and I have seen in those people the transformation, mainly emotional, of well-being (Fogo).
> [...] After the Community Therapy sessions, I learnt to listen more! [...] I learnt that people don't always have illnesses that are physical illnesses and that we have to take care, yes take care of body, mind and soul! We have to listen!" (Water).
> With regard to the most significant changes, I can say that listening is very significant [...] And humanisation! I think that when you listen you're already treating with humanisation, and it's already a way of valuing the other person, because when you cut off speech, you're devaluing the other person [...] You learn to contain yourself!" (Céu).
> I learnt to love more, to understand more and to be more affectionate! Because I imagine it like this: we give what we receive [...] So in Community Therapy it's a pleasant circle, there's that wonderful human cosiness that you feel that affection that's not an affection that you're giving out of obligation [...] In Community Therapy it's not like that. I feel that the therapist who conducts the Community Therapy circle doesn't do it for the sake of doing it [...] She passes on that human warmth, affection, cosiness, good feeling (Montanha).

In his research, Guimarães (2006) states that the paradigms of complexity and systemic vision help to understand the problem situations presented in Community Therapy meetings, since they perceive the individual as a whole, inserted in a social and family system, paying attention to their relationships with the other elements of this system.

For Barreto (2008), the secret of the systemic approach lies in establishing relationships. Everything is a relationship. Nothing has meaning or significance when seen in isolation. Elements come together not by chance, but according to their own logic, and Community Therapy, anchored in systemic thinking, breaks away from the vertical model in which everyone only understands the part, the element, to a model in which everything and everyone is involved. The wheels are not intended to leave people with all the issues resolved, but with questions that can result in a new way of looking at the problem, which may even point to a new solution and offer an opportunity for permanent growth and transformation.

Community therapy is an instrument that enables the development of humanised relationships, helping to build bonds between participants, and so open, frank dialogue in a climate of respect for expressions, feelings and emotions seems to facilitate the building of supportive bonds. Being able to talk in a group, release tensions and be welcomed frees people up to establish healthier relationships without fear of judgement (BARRETO, 2008).

Community therapy is an instrument for building social networks of solidarity to promote life and mobilise the resources and skills of individuals, families and communities. Community therapy invites us to change our outlook and focus, without wishing to disqualify the contributions of other approaches, but by broadening its angle of action.

As Barreto (2008) states, it is Brazil's cultural diversity that makes this country great. Enabling everyone to add new values is an invaluable asset in the process of "empowerment" and the construction of citizenship.

Therefore, leaving isolation and limitations in search of the collective, as well as reaching out to the community, brings to a movement all the possibilities revealed at the disposal of a new action, rescuing and valuing customs, values, beliefs, life stories, knowledge, in short, culture, sometimes forgotten or little valued, but which there, in the circle, emerges with new power inspiring or revealing itself as valuable therapeutic resources.

Community therapy awakens positive thoughts about the person and their relationship with the world, revitalising their capacity to react and mobilising vital energies in order to bring about an integral transformation (physical, mental, emotional, spiritual and social) in personal and social aspects (BARRETO, 2008).

In the narratives of the collaborators, the contribution of the Community Therapy circles on doing well for oneself is clear, as shown in the following statement:

> The changes that I consider most significant, apart from this attitude, are the results that I see on a daily basis, in the practice of exercising... Because Community Therapy has brought me, as a health professional, another proposal for care that isn't just that moment in the rodas and forget about it (Fogo).

Barreto (2008) says that this way of working allows progress to be made from the pathology-centred model to the model of health promotion, solidarity networks and social inclusion. Based on these principles, the problem situations chosen by the participants in the circle to be worked on favour the growth of the individual and the people closest to them, in the sense of nurturing the growth of autonomy, awareness and co-responsibility.

As a result, it can be seen that the experience of Community Therapy circles brought about significant changes in the lives of all the collaborators who took part in this study.

5.2. COMMUNITY THERAPY WHEELS AND THE (RE)SIGNIFICATION OF PROFESSIONAL PRACTICES

According to Silva (2009), one of the many challenges to be overcome in order to continue the complex and exhausting mission of building the SUS is the humanisation of care. Humanisation is understood as dignity and respect for the inalienable rights of the population to be well looked after, as well as the responsibility and commitment of the health team to solve the health problems of the people under their care.

According to Rocha (2009), for there to be a change in the way health professionals carry out their practices, it is essential to dialogue, problematise and reflect on events related to people's lives and within the services, on what needs to be improved. As such, it is necessary to promote changes in relationships, in health acts and, above all, in people, transforming hegemonic practices with a view to building new knowledge and doing innovative things collectively.

According to Campos (2003), it is the ESF's job to support users with a view to broadening their capacity to think, enabling them to acquire empowerment so that they can exercise greater control over their lives. He argues that this would be an important step in bringing team members and users closer together, with positive repercussions on the way health is produced and the quality of the service offered.

As a result of taking part in the Community Therapy sessions, the outlook of the collaborators in this study was broadened in the sense of valuing the individual and restoring autonomy, because, as Barreto (2008) states, each person has a life experience and should be encouraged to be co-responsible for the suffering of others. Not as a "saviour of the fatherland", giving advice and exhortations, but by sharing their pain, their difficulties, their discoveries, in a simple way, opening their heart and showing solidarity with the appeals of others. Thus, the narratives of the collaborators show that Community Therapy has contributed to transforming the practices of the professionals taking part in the round tables, according to the following examples:

> [...] And as a Community Health Agent, I've brought Community Therapy to me as another tool, another piece of work material, on home visits, on how to deal with families, with the problems I encounter on a daily basis. So Community Therapy is a key point for me, another learning experience in life and in my profession!" (Montanha).
>
> [...] I've also learnt a lot as a health professional to listen to people as a whole, because sometimes a person just needs a word, to be heard [...] I consider these to be the most significant changes: Learning to listen, to respect, to look after people as a whole [...] The mind and the soul too, which is the most important thing! (Water).
>
> [...] Because Community Therapy has brought me, as a health professional, another proposal for care that isn't just that moment in the circles and forget about it [...] (Fogo).
>
> From the moment I took part in the Community Therapy circles, the change in my work process was inevitable because I began to realise when I tried to put myself in the user's shoes [...] How difficult it is [...] Would I want to arrive at a Family Health Unit and be told no, straight away? (Lago).

According to Fortes and Martins (2004), humanisation in health rescues the individuality of each person, gives them the opportunity to share in decision-making regarding their health and expands the possibilities for autonomy.

In her research, Rocha (2009) found that the participation of health professionals in the Community Therapist training process provided greater contact between them (Community Therapists) and the community, as it guaranteed them a space to speak and listen. In this research, the narratives express changes in day-to-day work, revealing welcoming practices between professionals and users, as the following statements show:

> [...] you can associate this with welcoming, with how to welcome people, because in Community Therapy you welcome so well [...] Everyone identifies themselves, says what they bring and in the end the person also says what they are taking away from that experience, from that round of conversation, and welcoming is a conversation that we have with the user (Céu).
>
> Through Community Therapy, I realise that a fundamental part of this whole story has also been in relation to welcoming, trying to listen to others, putting yourself in their shoes as you would like to be welcomed [...] And so, I've learned a lot (Lago).
>
> In my work process, I realise that the biggest influence is valuing listening to people, people in a hurry: "What now? Are we going to medicate straight away?" No. It was already a habit of mine to try and listen, but I've really valued what people have said even more, not just me but all the professionals who are part of the Family Health Team... (Fogo).

According to Cecílio (2001), comprehensive care, in the singular space of the health service, could be defined as the effort of the health team to translate and meet, in the best possible way, the needs of users captured in their individual expression, and as a result have the product of the effort of each of the workers and the team as a whole. To achieve this, the challenge must be overcome in the service management process, particularly in the processes of conversation and communication - understanding for action - that are established between the different health workers.

In this sense, this study identifies changes in relations between professionals in favour of interaction between them, as exemplified below:

> I kiss the receptionist, the cleaner, the doctor, the nurse, I don't differentiate between people [...] Whoever doesn't like me, it's not my fault, but I give them the best of what I've learnt [...] (Montanha).
>
> [...] I can say that Community Therapy helps professionals to relate to each other, to be together in a place like my unit, for example, where there are four Family Health Teams working together [...] (Céu).
>
> [...] More companionship, more dedication, more commitment is what everyone has today here in this Health Unit [...] And before the Community Therapy circles, we went through times of turbulence where no one understood anyone [...] (Vento).
>
> [...] There was a rapprochement with the team, a greater understanding with others and, consequently, a broader vision to understand the work of others, and hence this integration in the work process (Trovão).
>
> With regard to the work process in the Family Health Strategy, before the Community Therapy sessions, the team's relationship at work was very difficult because people were more individualistic and since the Community Therapy sessions, there has been more affective contact and the relationship has improved between the professionals [...] We would arrive [...] Hug [...] Say good morning with a smile! (Água).

In view of the experiences of the collaborators in this research, the Community Therapy circles have given them a new perspective, a new way of acting, a new way of practising their profession, of turning towards others, and have revealed a change in practices, an invitation to be and to grow personally and professionally. This observation is noteworthy because nowadays it is worth observing the consequences/effects of the Community Therapy circles, given that we are still facing institutional autism, the difficulties of acting in a resolutive manner and involved in the defence of life, sometimes contaminated by deviations in training that lead to the fragmentation and parcelling out of care tasks in such a way that acting becomes merely a distant and automated technical act. In this study, we can see from the collaborators' revelations that the Community Therapy circles have led to changes in the health team's daily routine in the sense that they point towards building healthy bonds between professionals and users, bringing affection to the work and making it more human, as exemplified by the following narratives:

> I think the most significant change in my work is being able to help others, even with a hug, or even with a smile [...] Today I speak more softly, I speak more kindly to people, I'm more patient, I know how to listen to people more, how to hug, how to feel the other person!
>
> [...] there in the circle I believe it creates a better bond of affection [...] That we stop! [...] Give hugs! [...] You get to know the problem the other person is going through [...] (Water).
>
> [...] That way of hugging [...] The way everyone hugs, sings and dances together breaks a tremendous ice in our lives when we're taking part in the Community Therapy circle [...] (Céu).

The SUS, characterised by the generosity of its actions, was not a concession by government officials, but a conquest by Brazilians in the midst of an intense movement of struggles and social mobilisation, so respecting this right is the obligation of health managers and workers and nothing justifies poor service by a health service.

Community therapy groups are an important space for participation, as they offer individuals the chance to listen and be listened to, to reflect and to act. According to Barreto (2008), it's a time when you can examine your life and motivations in depth; when you can learn from each other's experiences and thus find solutions to your own problems. It takes humility and awareness to realise that power does not lie with those who know how to manipulate words and people, but in the hands of those who know how to listen, share, stimulate, integrate and who want to participate.

In his study, Holanda (2006) states that Community Therapy can be recommended as a community health action, to be included in the SUS primary care network, and can be included on the agenda of health units, as it provides welcome, mobilises the community, strengthens bonds, builds webs of solidarity and favours communication between popular and scientific knowledge.

In this sense, the Family Health Teams, whose task is to offer humanised, comprehensive and quality care to all those under their responsibility, according to a territorial and health focus, need to realise that this task will only be possible if there is a willingness to produce care that goes beyond technique, medicalisation and procedures, incorporating the subjective dimensions of workers and users. The following statements reveal changes that include subjectivity from the perspective of producing comprehensive and humanised care:

> [...] I feel I've had a change in the way I work [...] In the way I practice my profession, in the way I take care of users, in home visits, because they're tiring [...] We go up and down hills and deal with people in all kinds of ways [...] And that's why I say that the most important thing I've acquired is precisely that: patience to deal with these situations and practice my profession (Terra).
>
> I have a different perspective now [...] I can see a person, not by what they're saying, but let's see what they're going through, and why they're like that [...] And sometimes I used to ignore why that person was in a bad mood because I can act one way and that person can't [...] They can be going through a season of life and I can't understand it [...] (Vento).
>
> If we don't manage to establish a rapport with the user, in other words, a good welcome, treating them with consideration, as if they really are a human being, worthy, and that the SUS is also worthy, you can't get them to feel a certain intimacy with you and it's just that technical professional/user relationship [...] It's over there, it's dead [...] And I realise that Community Therapy taught me this too: to listen; when you arrive, ask their name, call them by their name [...] (Céu).
>
> When I arrive at a house where the person needs to talk [...] If I realise that they need it [...] I listen [...] It's happened that I've arrived and thought that my visit was going to be simple, because that family never had any problems and the lady was in great need [...] She was having a lot of difficulties with her husband, with her marriage and all that confusion [...] It ended up that I was there almost all morning listening... (Water).

For Gadamer (2002), the production of sharing between health professionals and users must go beyond listening to what the other person demanding care says about what the professional needs to know, in other words, it is also necessary to listen to what is essential for both to know so that existing technical resources can be used to achieve the desired success.

According to Barreto (2008), reflection on the social problems that affect individuals moves from the private sphere to public, collective and community sharing. The emphasis on group work, so that together they can share problems and solutions and act as a protective shield for the most vulnerable, are instruments for social aggregation and insertion.

By affirming that the solution lies in the collective and its interactions, in sharing, in identifying with the other, in respecting differences, professionals must be part of this construction. Both benefit: the community generates autonomy and social insertion and the professionals are cured of their "institutional and professional autism", as well as their alienation from the university.

In this way, the health professionals who collaborated in this study attested to changes that revealed humanised attitudes towards users, as can be seen in the following statements:

> I learnt in the Community Therapy sessions that we have to take care of our souls, and I believe that just stopping, listening and letting off steam is significant, because when someone has a problem, sometimes what they want most is for someone else to stop and listen [...] (Water).
> The most significant change I think is having a view of the human being as a whole, and that it's not just at that moment, but at various moments, wherever you are, having this view and this flexibility, being flexible especially when you're in contact with the user, with the professional and with the agendas relating to the work process (Lago).
> These are things that we might think have nothing to do with it, but they do, because when you welcome a person well, you realise that they are disarmed, they are completely at ease with you, talking to you [...] And if you welcome the user well, they are more comfortable talking to you, to have an exchange with you, not just a health-disease exchange, but an individual, personal exchange, to talk about something personal, you know? (Céu).

According to Rocha (2009), Community Therapy is a valuable tool within the work process that contributes to the construction of a humanised health model, expanding the caring dimension and reorienting the practices of SUS workers towards comprehensive care.

According to Ayres (2004), an apparently simple resource, but one that is little used in the relationship between professionals and users, can be to ask questions that are effectively interested in the other and to listen attentively and disarmingly to the otherness encountered.

The aforementioned author also states that other forms of non-verbal communication are also relevant to facilitating the caregiver encounter and cites as an example the power of the gaze that professionals experience when they hear something from someone seeking their care, and perceive very different things when they look at them.

The Humanisation of Care in the SUS involves the creation of new standards of relationship between workers and users and the implementation of new management practices.

And so, our way of touching, our body posture, our gestures, the attitudes of responsibility, welcome and commitment that we demonstrate with our actions, the environment in which we find ourselves, all these aspects must be remembered when it comes to enhancing dialogue in the caring encounter (AYRES, 2004).

In this study, the collaborators revealed the contributions of Community Therapy in their processes of change at work, as revealed in the following reports:

> In my work process, I realise that the greatest influence is the appreciation of listening to people... Because Community Therapy has

> brought me, as a health professional, another proposal for care that isn't just for that moment in the circles and forget about it [...] (Fogo).
> [...] And they don't tell everyone on the street about their problems because they have to have confidence [...] And in Community Therapy circles, the space passes on this confidence and the person who takes part knows that what they say will remain with the professionals who are there. It really helps!" (Água).

It is interesting to note that Holanda (2006), in his study, states that Community Therapy allows the health team to understand the diversity of cultural values in which the Family Health Unit (USF) is inserted, developing health promotion activities, rescuing citizenship and providing comprehensive care to the clientele.

As Barreto (2008) states, it's not a question of rejecting scientific knowledge, but of rescuing this other source of competence. It's about allowing a scientific method to enable the other, more intuitive and cultural method, to take shape, awareness, consistency and recognition of skills acquired in ways other than conventional ones. This means recognising that culture also has its processes and methods for generating skills and competences.

According to Oliveira and Marcon (2007), in the field of primary care, the user must be approached in their socio-economic and cultural context, recognised and valued as an autonomous subject, and it is up to the team to create conditions and encourage their participation in their work processes.

In this study, the statements below reaffirm this understanding:

> [...] Because Community Therapy in this process of humanisation brings the community closer to the unit and the unit closer to the community because we notice that sometimes the community wants to get closer, but the unit distances itself, and Community Therapy has played such an important role for the Family Health Unit in this rapprochement (Trovão).
> In the Community Therapy circles, we learn that it's important for people to identify themselves and be treated as the human being they are [...] The hug... That way of hugging [...] The way everyone hugs, sings and dances together breaks a tremendous ice in our lives when we're taking part in the Community Therapy circle [...] (Céu).

According to Barreto (2005), the educational process proposed by Paulo Freire, in which as one teaches, one also learns, making communication possible between popular knowledge and scientific knowledge and encouraging participation as a fundamental requirement for boosting social relations, supports the idea that promoting awareness and encouraging the group, through dialogue and reflection, to take initiatives and be agents of their own transformation, enables health professionals to use Community Therapy circles to grow collectively.

According to Holanda (2006), Community Therapy can be recommended as a community health action to be included in the SUS primary care network, and can be included on the agenda of health units, as it provides a welcoming atmosphere, mobilises the community, strengthens bonds, builds webs of solidarity and favours communication between popular and scientific knowledge.

In this sense, the collaborators in this study refer to the influence of participation in Community Therapy circles on doing good for themselves and for others, also revealing an expansion of the caring dimension that is essential and necessary for those who dedicate themselves to caring for other human beings with feelings and emotions who seek, in the encounter with a health professional or service, possibilities for care that meets their needs.

Community therapy circles enable relationships to be horizontal and, as Paulo Freire (1996) said: In this place of encounter, there are no absolute ignoramuses, nor absolute sages; there are men who, in communion, seek to know more. And so, in the stories told, the collaborators refer to changes in work processes, as the following statements say:

> Bringing this into the work process, I realise that you also have to break the ice [...] The ice of indifference, the ice of the user thinking or us thinking that we're wiser, or that we're more intelligent than them, or that we're more empowered by scientific knowledge and we look down on the user, but they also have knowledge [...] They also have knowledge about herbs, teas and things they know, but sometimes they're looked down on or despised [...] (Céu).
>
> It was already a habit of mine to try and listen, but I've really valued what people have said even more, not just me but all the professionals who are part of the Family Health Team [...] We really try to sit down, listen, really let people talk... And there are consultations that used to last five minutes and now last fifteen or twenty [...] Just the person sitting down, talking... (Fogo).

For Baremblitt (2002), the health worker operates their cognitive dimension, that of being a worker endowed with full technical capacity to intervene in health problems, and also operates a subjective dimension, that of being for themselves and the other, conferring alterity in the acts of care, where the other is always present as a subject in the action of producing care.

Welcoming, recognising and giving the necessary support to those experiencing suffering provides greater humanisation of relationships, as stated by Barreto (2008), and bringing this reflection to the work process of family health teams, it is understood that Community Therapy has contributed to re-signifying the way in which the professionals who took part in this study refer to the relationship with users, getting involved, respecting, seeking to understand their health needs from the perspective of comprehensive care, as stated by the collaborators below:

> [...] There are the difficulties of the health professional who always wants to medicalise all people's pain [...] And often forgets that a simple attitude of listening, and hearing what your neighbour wants and feels, already brings about a great transformation for those who speak, and this has also changed the way I look at people (Fogo).
>
> [...] Wherever you are, have that look and that flexibility, be flexible especially when you're in contact with the user, with the professional and with the agendas, the agendas relating to the work process (Lago).
>
> And the Community Therapy sessions have been important for the user I'm visiting, because I've gained experience in dealing with this, I've learnt not to advise anyone, and there are people who don't like advice, but I've learnt to tell them a story, I say: look, I'm going to tell you a story that's more or less identical to yours, you know? (Vento).
>
> [...] I feel I've had a change in the way I work [...] In the way I practice my profession, in the way I take care of users, in home visits, because they're tiring [...] We go up and down hills and deal with people in all kinds of ways [...] And that's why I say that the most important thing I've acquired is precisely that: patience to deal with these situations and practice my profession (Terra).
>
> I learnt in the Community Therapy sessions that we have to take care

> of our souls, and I believe that just stopping, listening and letting off steam is significant, because when someone has a problem, sometimes what they want most is for someone else to stop and listen [...] (Water).

According to Boff (2008), the rescue of care does not come at the expense of work, but through a different way of understanding and carrying out work. To do this, human beings need to turn inward and discover their way of being cared for.

For the author mentioned above, caring is more than an act, it is an attitude that encompasses more than a moment of attention, zeal and care. It represents an attitude of occupation, concern, responsibility and emotional involvement with the other. It is through caring for others that human beings develop the dimension of otherness, respect and the fundamental values of the human experience.

The philosopher Martin Heidegger, in his work *Being and Time,* refers to care as a phenomenon that is the enabling basis of human existence as a human being, so, since care is in the nature and constitution of the human being, without care the human being ceases to be human.

Faced with this way of perceiving the human being, health professionals involved in the defence of life must be understood as subjects who take care of themselves and others as unequivocal conditions for justifying their existence and being able, every day, to produce and reproduce life with pleasure and professional fulfilment, so that when they take care of others, they understand that even before satisfying the needs of others, they are responding to their own human needs. As the statements below illustrate, the collaborators in this study have broadened their vision of existence:

> The most significant change I consider is when you look at the human being as a whole (Lago).
>
> I believe that the most significant change is this question of feeling more human. Community therapy leads to a very humanising process (Trovão).
>
> So I think Community Therapy [...] My God in heaven [...] It's done so many things! It's about treating others as human beings, as you would like to be treated [...] (Céu).

And it's worth remembering what Barreto (2008) says, that it's not possible to imagine that the working or living conditions of employees have changed, because the actual time of participation is too short for there to be a change in material conditions; in reality, it's people's worldviews that have changed.

Learning that she is not alone, that she has the capacity to re-signify that feeling, to transform her pain into a source of overcoming and to face her difficulties with a different outlook based on a re-reading of the contextualised reality.

Reality is a university and teaches us at every moment to relativise the knowledge we have built up in order to include other knowledge built up in other contexts. The same author says that Community Therapy, like any integrative approach, knows that it is possible to transform the shock and pain of this confrontation into something creative, integrated and built collectively.

In this way, this study recorded the experience of the Community Therapy circles, contributing to institutional changes in the work processes of ESF professionals based on the lessons learnt collectively.

CHAPTER 6

6. FINAL CONSIDERATIONS

This study was inspired by my desire and curiosity as a health professional to understand the changes brought about by participation in Community Therapy circles among professionals in the Family Health Strategy, involving both the personal and professional dimensions. In order to make this research possible, the methodological approach of Thematic Oral History was chosen, and it was carried out with the valuable collaboration of eight collaborators from different professional categories in the Family Health Strategy.

It is important to note that the knowledge of the collaborators' life stories, captured during the interviews and through the notes in the field diary, led the master's student to take a look at her own practice. As well as achieving the research objectives, this also helped the researcher to reconnect with herself, realising that she takes care of others because she needs to take care of herself. And so, as in a movement of harmony between work and care, each health professional can and should take on the role of active subject of their history and guarantee their place as a human being who works and cares, allowing themselves to feel human and remain human by existing fully.

In the narratives, the collaborators revealed that Community Therapy, as a tool for caring, contributes significantly to bringing the worlds of work and life closer together and, in this sense, the change in professional practice is clear in the statements of all the collaborators, since, by reflecting on aspects of their life stories in a movement rocked by the rhythm of the other human being, they re-signified individual/private and collective/social aspects, starting to adopt a different way of caring for others, acting positively within a new ethic with life and the profession.

Another aspect worth highlighting is the process of reorganising primary care, which can trigger changes at other levels of the health system. Hence Community Therapy's potential to contribute to changes in the work process of Family Health Strategy professionals within a new care model format.

Being able to feel that the participants in the Community Therapy circles, as was the case with the collaborators in this study, who bring other perspectives to other humans, promoting a recovery of distanced humanity, was revealing of the impact that Community Therapy had on the transformation of those who understood that caring for the other takes care of themselves in a relationship of therapeutic healing for the other, because when she was welcomed in her suffering, she learnt to welcome the service user and try to understand what their needs are and what lies beyond their speech, translated into a symptom or even gestures and expressions of aggression that they sometimes experience.

The opportunity to carry out this study exceeded the initial expectations of the master's student, who believes that acting in the face of oneself and the other is inseparable and who had never understood how some professionals did not take co-responsibility for the care they produced, which reinforces the contribution of Community Therapy as another powerful tool to be recommended whenever there is a willingness to create and recreate ways of collectively producing ways of defending individual and collective life with an integrative, holistic, humanised, democratic, free practice, without side effects, as another collaborator in this study said.

Community therapy, as an opportunity for personal and professional growth and development, helped to incorporate this care technology to be used as another way of learning about life and work in order to deal with concerns, insofar as it became a space for sharing experiences and producing skills for new ways of acting, because it took on a new meaning.

As a care tool for the work process of ESF health professionals, the research presented here recommends expanding the training of community therapists in the Family Health Strategy, with the possibility of increasing access to this device by more professionals, and it can be used in any type of service and by any type of group, including being expanded in health services other than Primary Care.

It is known that the challenges that are part of the daily lives of health workers require the incorporation of "raw material" that is not exclusive to the ESF, given that various obstacles are present in spaces other than Family Health Units, as a result of the difficulties that need to be overcome in the health system as a whole and that directly affect the lives of workers. Therefore, being able to rely on a powerful strategy to care for them mobilises renewed energy.

In this sense, Community Therapy can be used as a working tool in places where health professionals want to change their practices, pointing to the possibility of changes in their work processes.

The narratives were revealing of the process of transformation that took place with each person at their own time, with one collaborator revealing that he had noticed a change in his personal life after taking part in the first Community Therapy circle, as well as other significant changes, such as overcoming fears, reviewing concepts, re-signifying the work that had previously been carried out without reflection, but that, motivated by the experiences in the circles, listening to the other and to himself, it was possible to understand where some of the demands come from with regard to the needs of the users who come to them.

The changes resulting from participation in the Community Therapy circles were part of the examples of a new way of acting revealed by the health professionals in their day-to-day visits, consultations, meetings and scheduling, moving them from a position of technician, driven by learned knowledge, but now (re)meaningful, helping these new subjects to produce comprehensive and humanised care for users.

Community therapy can be a way of instituting changes in health care, in the areas of promotion and prevention, rescuing fundamental concepts of bonding, humanisation, co-responsibility and resolutiveness that point to a reorientation of the way health services operate.

Based on this study, it is necessary to carry out further research into the subject, as well as looking for other references to establish a new perspective on the health work process and the challenges needed to build a new way of doing things in defence of life and the SUS.

The dissemination of this experience helps health professionals to recognise the importance of Community Therapy as an instrument for mobilising personal and cultural resources to build social support networks for health promotion, in line with the principles of the SUS.

From this perspective, Community Therapy, by making it possible to get to know the participants' life stories, can contribute to an invitation to think about the way humans are as a continuous conception/realisation of a project that finds in existential phenomenology the key that opens up as a way to understand the health professional as a subject, since as well as being a health worker, they are a human person, an active and participating subject with their way of being in the world, singular, plural, in relation to other subject(s).

In this way, it also works as a strategy for mental health care in primary care for users and primary care workers so that they can enhance their actions, enabling the construction of community-based social solidarity networks to resolve conflicts, both for ESF users and professionals.

REFERENCES

ABRATECOM - **Brazilian Association of Community Therapy**. Available at: <www.abratecom.org.br>. Accessed on: Oct. 2009.

ANDRADE, L.O.M.; BARRETO, I.C.H.C.; BARRETO, A.P.; OLIVEIRA, M.V. **O SUS e a terapia comunitária.** UFC Fortaleza, 2009.

AYRES, J. R. C. M. Hermeneutics and the humanisation of Health Practices. **Ciência & Saúde Coletiva,** v. 10, n. 3, p. 549-560, 2005.

AYRES, J. R. C. M. O cuidado, os modos de ser (do) humano e as práticas de saúde. **Saúde e Sociedade,** v. 13, n. 3, p. 16-29, 2004.

BAREMBLITT, G. **Compendium of institutional analysis**. Belo Horizonte: Félix Guattari Institute, 2002.

BARRETO, A. P. **Terapia comunitária passo a passo**. Fortaleza: Gráfica LCR, 2005.

____. **Community therapy step by step.** Fortaleza: Gráfica LCR, 2008.

BERTONCINI, J. H. **Da intenção ao gesto uma análise da implantação do Programa de Saúde da Família em Blumenau** (Master's dissertation). Florianópolis: Department of Public Health, Federal University of Santa Catarina, 2000.

BOAS, F. **Cultural anthropology**. Rio de Janeiro: Jorge Zahar, 2004.

BOFF, L. **Saber cuidar, ética do humano** - Compaixão pela terra, 15. ed. Petrópolis, RJ, Editora Vozes, 2008.

BOM MEIHY, J. C. S. HOLANDA, F. **História oral:** como fazer como pensar. São Paulo: Editora Contexto, 2007.

BOM MEIHY, J. C. S. **Manual de história oral**. 5. ed. São Paulo: Loyola, 2005.

BRAZIL. Ministry of Health. **Ordinance No. 196/96.** Provisions on research involving human beings. Brasília, DF, 1996.

. Ministry of Health. **Ordinance No. 648** of 28 March 2006. Approves the National Primary Care Policy. Brasília, DF, 2006.

____. Ministry of Health. Health Care Secretariat. DAPI. **Mental Health in the SUS:** access to treatment and changing the model of care. Management Report 2003-2006. Brasília, DF, 2007.

. Ministry of Health. **Panel of SUS indicators N° 4.** Brasília, DF, 2008.

____. Ministry of Health. **Revista Brasileira**, Saúde da Família, Saúde da Família nos Territórios da Cidadania-Ano IX- April to June 2008, Brasília, DF, 2008.

____. Ministério da Saúde **Revista Brasileira**, Saúde da Família, Práticas Integrativas e Complementares em Saúde: Uma Realidade no SUS -Ano IX- Maio de 2008, Brasília, DF, 2008. Special edition.

____. Ministry of Health. Approves the National Policy for Integrative and Complementary Practices (PNPIC) in the single health system. **Ordinance no. 971,** of 3rd May 2006. Available at: <portal.saude.gov.br/portal/arquivos/pdf/PNPIC.pdf>. Accessed on: 10 August 2009.

____. Ministry of Health. **National Policy for Integrative and Complementary Practices in the SUS-PNPIC.** ATTITUDE TO EXPANDING ACCESS. Series B. Basic Health Texts. Brasília- DF, 2008.

. Ministry of Health. **National Humanisation Policy** - Base Document. Brasilia, 2006.

CAIRO, C. **Language of the body:** learn to listen to it for a healthy life. São Paulo: Mercuryo, 1999.

CAMPINAS. Municipal Health Department. **Base text for discussion on**

Matriciamento. Campinas, 2004.
CAMPOS, C.E.A. O desafio da integralidade segundo as perspectivas da vigilância da saúde e da saúde da família. **Journal Ciência e Saúde Coletiva**, 8(2). 2003.
CAMPOS, G. W. S. Paidéia e modelo de atenção: um ensaio sobre a reformulação do modo de produzir saúde. **Olho Mágico**, v.10, n.2, apr./jun.,2003.
CAMPOS, M.D.; MENDES, M.S.F.; ABREU, G.R.S.; BESSAS, D.E.C.; SOARES,G.nN.; VIEIRA, L.J. Reflexões acerca do acolhimento em uma unidade básica de saúde de Belo Horizonte, Minas Gerais. In: **Saúde em Debate.** Journal of the Brazilian Centre for Health Studies. Rio de Janeiro, v 31 n. 75/76/77 jan./dez.2007.
CAPRA, F. **The web of life:** a new scientific understanding of living systems. São Paulo: Cultrix Publishing House, 2000.
CARMELLO, E. **Resilience:** Managing adverse and high-pressure situations. Available at: http://www.entheusiasmos.com.br/. Accessed on 12 August 2009.
CECÍLIO, L.C.O. Health Needs as a Structuring Concept in the Struggle for Integrality and Equity in Health Care. In: PINHEIRO, R.; MATTOS, R.A. (eds). **The meanings of comprehensiveness in health care**. Rio de Janeiro: Abrasco, 2001.
CORRÊA, A. F. **Virtual anthropology community.** Available at: <http//www.antropologia.com.br/colu/colu10.htm>. Accessed on: 21 Nov. 2007.
DEMO, P. **Introduction to sociology:** complexity, interdisciplinarity and social inequality. São Paulo: Editora Atlas S.A., 2002.
DIAS, M. D. **Mãos que acolhem vidas**: as partes tradicionais no cuidado durante a nascimento em uma comunidade nordestina. 2002. 204f. Thesis (Doctorate in Nursing). School of Nursing, University of São Paulo, São Paulo, 2002.
FERREIRA, A.B.H. **Novo Aurélio Século XXI**: o dicionário da língua portuguesa. 3 ed. Rio de Janeiro: Nova Fronteira, 1999.
FERREIRA FILHA, M.O.; DIAS, M.D. **A terapia comunitária no contexto do sistema único de saúde - SUS** / UFPB - 2007.
FERREIRA FILHA, M.O. **Community therapy**: a basic mental health action. Extension Project (PROBEX), UFPB/CCS/DESPP. 2006.
FORTES, P.A.C.;MARTINS, C.L. A Ética, A Humanização e a Saúde da Família. **Revista Brasileira de Enfermagem**, Brasília, v.53, n. especial, p. 31-33, dez.2000.
FRANCISCONI, C.F.; GOLDIM, J.R. **Termo de consentimento informado para a pesquisa,** 2003. Available at: <http://www.ufrgs.br/bioetica/conspesq.htm>. Accessed on: Jul. 2009.
FRANCO, T.B. **Reestruturação produtiva e transição tecnológica na saúde**: um olhar a partir do Sistema Cartão Nacional de saúde. (Doctoral Thesis). DMPS/UNICAMP: Campinas (SP), 2003.
____. Networks in the Micropolitics of the Work Process. In: **Gestão em redes:** práticas de avaliação, formação e participação na saúde. Rio de Janeiro, 2006.
____. **Production of care and pedagogical production: integration of health system scenarios in Brazil.** *Interface (Botucatu)* [online]. 2007, vol.11, n.23, pp. 427-438.
FRANCO, T.B; MERHY. E.E. **PSF:** contradictions and new challenges. National Health Conference on-line Tribuna Livre. Belo Horizonte/Campinas. March 1999.
____. **The use of analysing tools to support the planning of health services:** the case of the social service of the Hospital das Clínicas da Unicamp (Campinas, SP). São Paulo: Hucitec, 2003.
FREESE, E. **Municípios:** a gestão da mudança em saúde. Recife: University Publishing House, 2004.

FREIRE, P. **Pedagogia da autonomia:** saberes necessárias à prática educativa. São Paulo: Paz e Terra, 1996.
FREIRE, P. **Pedagogy of the oppressed.** 41 ed. Rio de Janeiro: Paz e Terra, 2005.
GADAMER, H.G. **Afterword to the 3ª edition of Truth and method:** fundamental traits of a philosophical hermeneutics. In: Truth and Method II. Petrópolis: Vozes, 2002. p. 508-544.
GRANDESSO, M.A. Community therapy**:** a critical postmodern practice - theoretical and epistemological considerations. In: CONGRESSO BRASILEIRO DE TERAPIA COMUNITÁRIA, 3., 2005, Fortaleza. **Proceedings.** Fortaleza: Abratecom, 2005. p. 44-45. Round table.
GUIMARÃES, F.J. **Repercussões da Terapia Comunitária no cotidiano de seus participantes**. 2006. 132f. Dissertation (Master's Degree) Health Sciences Centre, Federal University of Paraíba.
GUIMARÃES, F.J., FERREIRA FILHA, M.O. Repercussões da Terapia Comunitária no cotidiano de seus participantes. **Rev. Eletrônica Enfermagem**. v.8, n.3, p.404-414, 2006.
HEIDEGGER, M. **Being and Time**. Petrópolis; Vozes, 1995.
HOLANDA, V. R. **The contribution of community therapy to coping with the concerns of pregnant women.** - João Pessoa-PB, 2006. 140f Dissertation (Master's) - UFPB/CCS.
JOÃO PESSOA - PB. Municipal Health Department. **Municipal Health Plan** - Preliminary Version, 2006.
____. Municipal Health Department. **Health District II. Management Report.** 2008.
LAPLANTINE, F. **Learning anthropology**. São Paulo: Brasiliense, 1995.
LEAL, A.L. **ETD - Educação Temática Digital,** v.8, n.2, jun. 2007 - 205 Thematic Area: **Citizenship & Social Movements.**
LITLLEJONH, S. W. **Technical fundamentals of human communication**. Rio de Janeiro: Guanabara, 1998.
MATTOS, R.A. Integrality in practice (or about the practice of integrality). **Cadernos de Saúde Pública,** Rio de Janeiro, v.20, n.5, p.1411-1416, set./out.2004.
MERHY, E. E. In Search of Lost Time: the micropolitics of living labour in health. In: MERHY, E. E; ONOCKO, R. (Orgs.). **Acting in Health:** a challenge for the public. São Paulo: Hucitec; 1997.
MERHY, Emerson. **PSF:** contradictions and new challenges. Tribuna Livre, 1998.
____. **Health work.** São Paulo, 2003.
____. The act of caring: the soul of health services. In: BRAZIL. Ministry of Health. **Textbooks for the VER-SUS** Brazil **Pilot Project**. Brasília: MS, 2003.
MERHY, E.E; FRANCO,T.B. Family Health Programme: Are we for or against? **Saúde em Debate,** 26(60), p.118-122, 2002.
MERHY, E.E.; MAGALHAES JÚNIOR, H.M. et al. **O trabalho em saúde**: olhando e experienciando **o** SUS no cotidiano. São Paulo: Hucitec, 2003.
MINAYO, M.C.S. **O desafio do conhecimento**: pesquisa qualitativa em saúde. 10 ed. São Paulo: Hucitec, 2007.
MUNHOZ, M. L. P.; MALANGA, E. B. **Psychopedagogy and complex thinking.** Available at: <http://www.redebrasileiradetransdisciplinaridade.net/file.php/1/. Accessed on: 11 January 2010.
OLIVEIRA, D. G. S. **A história da terapia comunitária na atenção básica em João Pessoa - PB: uma ferramenta de cuidado**. 2008. 174 f. Dissertation (Master's Degree) Health Sciences Centre, Federal University of Paraíba.

OLIVEIRA, R. G.; MARCON, S.S. Working with families in the Family Health Programme: the practice of nurses in Maringá-Paraná. **Revista da Escola de Enfermagem- USP**, v.41, n.1, 2007.
PASELLO, A. **What is systems thinking?** Available at: <http://institutojetro.com.br/Lendoartigo.asp?a=939&T=2> Accessed on 11/Jan/2010.
PINHEIRO, D.P.N. A resiliência em discussão. **Psicologia em estudo**, v.9, n.1, p. 67-75, 2004.
PINHEIRO, R.; GUIZARDI, F.L. Cuidado e integralidade: por uma Genealogia de Saberes e Práticas no Cotidiano. In: PINHEIRO, R.; MATTOS, R.A. (eds). **Care at the frontiers of comprehensiveness.** Rio de Janeiro: Abrasco, 2008.
PINHEIRO, R.; MATTOS, R.A. (eds). **The meanings of comprehensiveness in health care**. Rio de Janeiro: Abrasco, 2001.
PIRES, D. Reestruturação produtiva e consequências para o trabalho em saúde. **Brazilian Journal of Nursing**, 2000.
PIRES, M. R. G. M.; DEMO, P. Políticas de saúde e crise do estado de bem-estar: Repercussões e possibilidades para o Sistema Único de Saúde. **Saúde soc**. 2006, v. 15, n. 2, p. 56-71.
RIBEIRO, E. M.; PIRES, D.; BLANK, V. L.G.: Theorising about the health work process as an instrument for analysing work in the Family Health Programme. **Cadernos de Saúde Pública** vol. 20 n. 2 Rio de Janeiro Mar/Apr. 2004.
ROCHA, E.F.L. **A terapia comunitária e as mudanças de práticas no SUS.** 2009.126f. Master's dissertation. UFPB/CCS- João Pessoa-PB.
SILVA, J.A.A. **SUS:** Navigating is necessary In: Brasil. Ministério da Saúde. 20 anos CONASEMS - Conselho Nacional de Secretarias Municipais de Saúde. Brasília-DF, 2009.
SOARES, C. S. D. A. **Terapia comunitária na estratégia saúde da família**: implicações no modo de andar a vida dos usuários. Ribeirão Preto-SP, 2008. Master's dissertation presented to the School of Nursing/USP. Ribeirão Preto-SP, 2008.
SOUSA, M. F. **Agentes comunitários de saúde:** Choque de Povo. São Paulo: Hucitec, 2003.
____. **A Cor-Agem do PSF**. 2. ed. São Paulo: Hucitec, 2003.
SPALTER, H; STREICHER, R.: **Practical and Quick FENG SHUI**. 8. ed. São Paulo: MADRAS, 2000.
VENTURA, C. Available at: <http://cantodofengshui.blogspot.com/2008/bagu.html.Acesso on 14 Feb.2010.
WATZLAWICK, P; HELMICK, J. H.B; JACKSON, D. **Pragmatics of human communication**. São Paulo: Cultrix, 1967.
WLASH, F. **Strengthening family resilience.** São Paulo: Rocca, 2005.

APPENDICES

APPENDIX A
FEDERAL UNIVERSITY OF PARAÍBA
HEALTH SCIENCES CENTRE
POSTGRADUATE PROGRAMME IN NURSING
INFORMED CONSENT FORM

Dear Sir or Madam:

This research, entitled RODAS DE TERAPIA COMUNITÁRIA: espaços de mudanças para profissionais da Estratégia Saúde da Família, is being carried out by Fernanda Lúcia de Sousa Leite Morais, a Master's student on the Postgraduate Nursing Programme at the Federal University of Paraíba (UFPB), under the supervision of Prof.ª Dr.ª Maria Djair Dias.

The aim of this study is to understand the changes that have taken place in the personal and professional dimensions of workers in the Family Health Strategy as a result of their experience in Community Therapy circles.

The aim of this research is to expand knowledge about Community Therapy, as well as to contribute, based on the knowledge produced, to the dissemination of new technologies that can be used as possibilities for changes in the work process involving professionals from the Family Health Strategy.

I would like to ask you to take part in an individual interview, using an MP3 recorder, in order to obtain the information necessary for the study. There will be no foreseeable risk to the interviewee.

In accordance with Resolution 196/1996 of the National Health Council on research involving human beings, the following will be guaranteed: information and clarification on any queries related to the research; the freedom to withdraw consent at any time and to stop taking part in the research without this causing any harm; the security of not being identified and the confidential nature of the information.

As well as permission to record the interview, I would also like to ask you to authorise me to present the results of this study at scientific events and in magazines or other media.

As a master's student, I am at your disposal for any clarification you may deem necessary at any stage of the research and I thank you for your co-operation.

In view of the above, I declare that I have been duly informed and give my consent to take part in the research and to publish the results. I am aware that I will receive a copy of this document.

João Pessoa, 2009

____

Signature of Research Participant

Signature of the Master's student in charge

Right thumb

APPENDIX B
FEDERAL UNIVERSITY OF PARAÍBA
HEALTH SCIENCES CENTRE
POSTGRADUATE PROGRAMME IN NURSING
LETTER OF ASSIGNMENT

João Pessoa, _____ 2009.

I, my marital status, identity document no., declare for all due purposes that I give up the rights to my interview, which has been transcribed, textualised, transcribed and authorised so that the Master's student Fernanda Lúcia de Sousa Leite Morais can use it in full or in parts, without restrictions on deadlines and citations, from the present date, in favour of her Master's dissertation, entitled: COMMUNITY THERAPY ROUTES: spaces for change for professionals in the Family Health Strategy.

In this way, I authorise their hearing and the use of quotes to third parties, as well as the dissemination of photographic images, with control being tied to the aforementioned researcher.

Giving up my rights and those of my descendants, I sign this document, which will have my signature notarised.

Signature of research collaborator

Signature of master's student

If you have any questions or need further clarification, please contact Fernanda Lúcia de Sousa Leite Morais (ID: 345611 SSP-PB). Address: Health Sciences Centre. University Campus I, João Pessoa-PB. CEP: 58059-900. Coordination of the Postgraduate Programme in Nursing at the Federal University of Paraíba-UFPB, João Pessoa-PB, Telephone: (83) 9107-4940; e-mail: fernandaleitemorais@gmail.com or with Professor Maria Djair Dias. Telephone: (83) 3216-7229.

APPENDIX C

FEDERAL UNIVERSITY OF PARAÍBA

HEALTH SCIENCES CENTRE

POSTGRADUATE PROGRAMME IN NURSING

Research title: COMMUNITY THERAPY WORKSHOPS: spaces for change for Family Health Strategy professionals.

Master's student: Fernanda Lúcia de Sousa Leite Morais

Supervisor: Prof.ª Dr.ª Maria Djair Dias

TECHNICAL FILE

IDENTIFICATION

- Name ______________________________
- Age ______________________________
- Profession ______________________________
- Workplace ______________________________
- Where you take part in TC ______________________________

CUTTING QUESTIONS:

1. Have there been any changes in your personal life since taking part in the Community Therapy sessions?
2. What change(s) have occurred in your work process as a result of taking part in the Community Therapy circles?
3. Which change(s) do you consider to be the most significant?

Table of contents

Printed by Books on Demand GmbH, Norderstedt / Germany